Ancient Greece

First published in Great Britain in 1997
by Macdonald Young Books an imprint of Wayland Publishers Limited
61 Western Road, Hove, East Sussex, BN3 1JD

Conceived and produced by Weldon Owen Pty Limited
43 Victoria Street, McMahons Point, NSW 2060, Australia
A member of the Weldon Owen Group of Companies
Sydney • San Francisco
Copyright ©1997 US Weldon Owen Inc.
Copyright © 1997 Weldon Owen Pty Limited

Chairman: Kevin Weldon
President: John Owen
Publisher: Sheena Coupe
Managing Editor: Rosemary McDonald
Project Editor: Ann B. Bingaman
Text Editors: Jane Bowring, Claire Craig
Art Director: Sue Burk
Designer: Avril Makula
Photo Research: Karen Burgess, Annette Crueger, Amanda Weir
Illustration Research: Peter Barker
Production Consultant: Mick Bagnato
Production Manager: Caroline Webber
Vice President International Sales: Stuart Laurence
Coeditions Director: Derek Barton

Text: Judith Simpson

Illustrators: Paul Bachem; Kenn Backhaus;
Chris Forsey; Adam Hook/Bernard Thornton Artists, UK;
Christa Hook/Bernard Thornton Artists, UK; Janet Jones;
Iain McKellar; Steve Noon/Garden Studio; Matthew Ottley;
Sharif Tarabay/Garden Studio; Steve Trevaskis;
Rod Westblade; Ann Winterbotham

A catalogue record for this book is available from the British Library

ISBN 0-7500-2375-9

Manufactured by Mandarin Offset
Printed in China

A Weldon Owen Production

Ancient Greece

CONSULTING EDITOR

Louise Schofield
Curator of Greek Bronze Age and Geometric Antiquities
Department of Greek and Roman Antiquities
British Museum, London

MACDONALD YOUNG BOOKS

Contents

• THE GREEK WORLD •

A Seafaring People	6
Early Settlements	8
The Mycenaeans	10
Settling New Lands	12
City-states	14
Government and the Law	16
On Mount Olympus	18
Stories of Daring Deeds	20
Crossing the River Styx	22

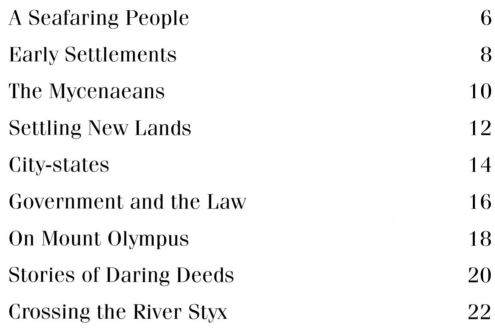

• LIVING IN ANCIENT GREECE •

In the Home	24
Writing and Education	26
Dressing for the Climate	28
Making a Living	30
Meeting Place	32
Eating and Drinking	34
Festival Games	36

• ARTS AND SCIENCE •

Thinking Things Through	38
Going to the Theatre	39
Sickness and Health	44
Clay and Metal	46
Building in Stone	48

• FOREIGN AFFAIRS •

Going to War	50
The Macedonians	52
The Hellenistic World	54
End of an Empire	56
Discovering Ancient Greece	58
Portraits from Ancient Greece	60
Glossary	62
Index	64

ITALY

IONIAN SEA

MACEDONIA

Mount Olympus ▲

Thermopylae ●

Delphi ●

Thebes ●

Marathon ●

Corinth ●

Athe

Olympia ●

Sparta ●

MEDITERRANEAN SEA

• THE GREEK WORLD •

A Seafaring People

The ancient Greek world took shape between 3200 and 1100 BC. This was during the Bronze Age when people first began melting copper with tin to make bronze. Island communities occupied the Cyclades and Crete, and the Mycenaean civilisation lived on mountainous mainland Greece. From the beginning, the ancient Greeks farmed the narrow valleys and coastal plains, wherever there was good soil and a river or a freshwater spring. Through the centuries, they cut trees from the mountain slopes for firewood and to build ships. They used ships more than any other means of transport, sailing the seas to trade, to go to war and to settle new places. Ancient Greek legends told of brave seafarers who survived dangerous voyages. Greece's boundaries expanded greatly from around 700 BC onward. Art and ideas developed strongly, and during the Hellenistic Age, the Greek way of life spread to many other countries.

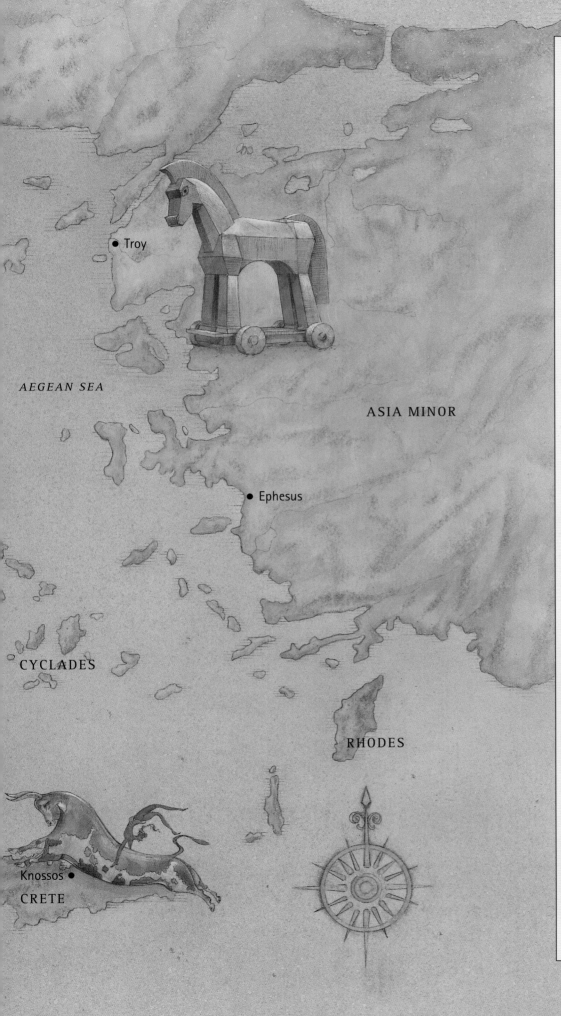

AEGEAN SEA

• Troy

ASIA MINOR

• Ephesus

CYCLADES

RHODES

Knossos •
CRETE

AGES OF ANCIENT GREECE

CYCLADIC CIVILISATION
3200–1100 BC
A Cycladic figurine of a harp player made from marble.

MINOAN CIVILISATION
3200–1100 BC

MYCENAEAN CIVILISATION
1600–1100 BC
A Mycenaean pottery cup decorated with a pattern of cuttlefish.

DARK AGE AND GEOMETRIC PERIOD
1100–700 BC

ARCHAIC PERIOD
700–480 BC
This Archaic bronze griffin's head was once attached to a large cooking pot.

CLASSICAL PERIOD
480–323 BC
A Classical red-figure vase showing Odysseus meeting a swineherd.

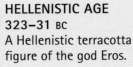

HELLENISTIC AGE
323–31 BC
A Hellenistic terracotta figure of the god Eros.

Discover more in End of an Empire

7

Early Settlements

FOLDED ARMS
Many marble figurines found on the Cyclades have the right arm folded below the left. The reason for this is unknown.

BULL LEAPING
Bulls were sacred animals to the Minoans. Young men and women leapt over them during religious ceremonies.

The first Greek civilisation was on a circle of small islands in the Aegean Sea called the Cyclades. The islanders grew grain, grapes and olives and raised animals for milk and meat. They produced clay pots and sculpted figurines out of marble, using blades and chisels made from hard volcanic rock and bronze. After many centuries, a disastrous earthquake followed by a huge volcanic explosion buried some Cycladic communities. On the large island of Crete to the south, however, other settlers were flourishing. Archaeologists have named these people after Minos, a legendary Cretan king. The Minoans built towns around large palaces and traded with many foreign countries. They invented a form of picture writing and then began to use symbols in a script archaeologists call Linear A. Mycenaeans on the nearby mainland later took over the island of Crete and became the most powerful people in the Aegean.

WALL PAINTING OF THE FLEET
At Akrotiri, on the Cycladic island of Thera, artists decorated the walls of many houses. This picture, painted around 1500 BC, is one of the best preserved.

SAILING AWAY
The painting tells the story of a sea voyage. The flagship (top centre) is carrying the leader of the expedition. Dolphins frolic around the boats in the calm water.

CUTTING EDGES
The double-headed axe was a sacred symbol in Minoan religion. It appeared on palace walls, pots and tombs.

KNOSSOS FRESCOES
The palace at Knossos was the largest palace on Crete. Built of stone and mud brick, it sprawled across a huge area. Wall paintings such as this have been restored to look as they once did.

MINOAN GODDESS
It is thought that the Minoans put goddesses above gods in their religion. This goddess, perhaps a protector of the household, holds a pair of sacred snakes.

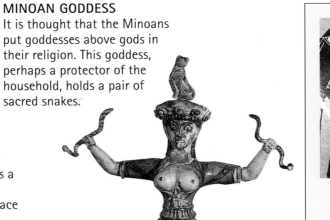

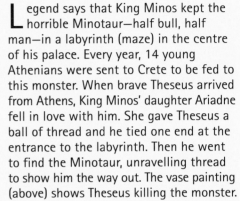

THE MINOTAUR

Legend says that King Minos kept the horrible Minotaur—half bull, half man—in a labyrinth (maze) in the centre of his palace. Every year, 14 young Athenians were sent to Crete to be fed to this monster. When brave Theseus arrived from Athens, King Minos' daughter Ariadne fell in love with him. She gave Theseus a ball of thread and he tied one end at the entrance to the labyrinth. Then he went to find the Minotaur, unravelling thread to show him the way out. The vase painting (above) shows Theseus killing the monster.

RETURNING HOME
The travellers are wearing Mycenaean armour and carrying Mycenaean weapons, so they may be returning to Mycenae on mainland Greece after visiting the Cyclades.

Discover more in Clay and Metal

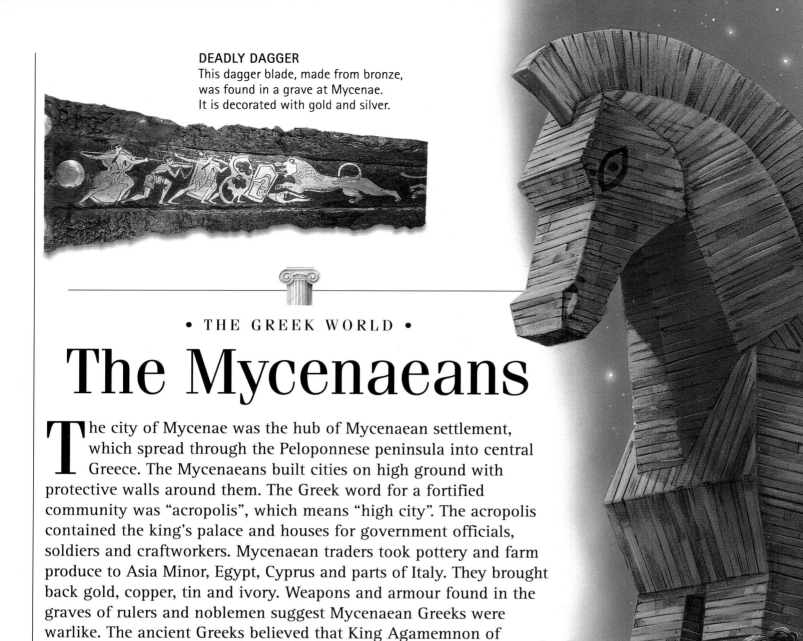

• THE GREEK WORLD •

The Mycenaeans

The city of Mycenae was the hub of Mycenaean settlement, which spread through the Peloponnese peninsula into central Greece. The Mycenaeans built cities on high ground with protective walls around them. The Greek word for a fortified community was "acropolis", which means "high city". The acropolis contained the king's palace and houses for government officials, soldiers and craftworkers. Mycenaean traders took pottery and farm produce to Asia Minor, Egypt, Cyprus and parts of Italy. They brought back gold, copper, tin and ivory. Weapons and armour found in the graves of rulers and noblemen suggest Mycenaean Greeks were warlike. The ancient Greeks believed that King Agamemnon of Mycenae led an army against the Trojans for the return of Helen, wife of his brother Menelaus. According to legend, the goddess Aphrodite encouraged Paris, a Trojan prince, to carry off Helen to his homeland. Myths about the heroes of the Trojan War were based on real events, and Troy was a real place in what is now Turkey. Around 1200 BC, Mycenae and neighbouring cities were violently destroyed. Archaeologists are not sure why this happened, but they know that Mycenaean civilisation ended soon afterwards.

MISTAKEN DATING
King Agamemnon supposedly led the Greek army against Troy. Archaeologist Heinrich Schliemann thought he had found the king's gold tomb mask at Mycenae. But this mask was made long before the Trojan War.

GIFT HORSE

After fighting the Trojans for ten years, the Greeks left a huge wooden horse outside Troy's walls and sailed away. The curious Trojans wheeled the statue into the city. That night, Greek soldiers hiding inside the hollow horse crept out and opened the gates. Their army, which had returned silently, entered Troy and defeated the Trojans.

SEARCHING FOR TROY

As a small boy, Heinrich Schliemann read about the Trojan War in Homer's *Iliad* and he vowed to find Troy. In 1870, relying on details from Homer's poem, Schliemann began to unearth a city at Hissarlik in Turkey. He discovered jewellery that he believed had belonged to Troy's King Priam. Nine cities lying on top of one another have since been found at Hissarlik. The city in the sixth layer is most likely to have been Troy.

Sophie Schliemann wearing jewellery excavated by her husband.

FRESCO AT MYCENAE

Frescoes are pictures painted on the walls of buildings while the plaster is still wet. These donkey-headed demons survive from the thirteenth century BC.

DID YOU KNOW?

Homer, a poet who lived in the eighth century BC, retold well-known Mycenaean legends in the *Iliad* and *Odyssey*. These long poems were possibly not written down until after Homer died.

MARINE THEME

The tentacles of an octopus writhe around this jar. Sea creatures, an important source of food, were popular in designs on Mycenaean pottery.

LIONS ON GUARD

The Lion Gate, named for the animals carved above it, was the main entrance to Mycenae. It was built about 1250 BC when the enormous stone city walls were increased in size.

Discover more in Stories of Daring Deeds

Settling New Lands

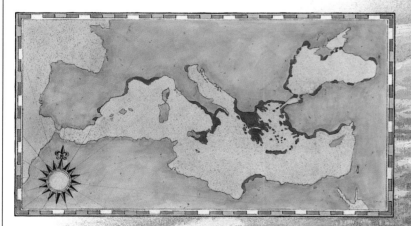

MINTED TO MATCH
Early silver coins from some southern Italian colonies had a raised design on one side and the reverse design on the other. These coins were very difficult to make.

When the Mycenaean civilisation ended, troubled times fell on ancient Greece. This period, now called the Dark Age, lasted about 400 years. It is thought that people forgot how to write because no writing has been found from this era. When food became scarce some people left their homeland to find new places to settle. They migrated to the coast of Asia Minor, stopping off at the Aegean Islands on the way. By the eighth century BC, Greece had recovered, but the growing population was overcrowding the mainland. Greek colonies spread around the Black Sea to the northeast, and west to southern Italy, and as far as France and Spain. Most colonies became farming communities, but a few were set up as trading posts. Successful settlements sent supplies back to Greece to relieve shortages there. The Black Sea ports exchanged grain and timber for wine, olive oil and honey.

GRIFFIN ON GUARD
Greek craftworkers sometimes learnt new skills from their neighbours. This griffin's head was made by bronze hollow casting, a method used in Asia Minor.

A RING OF COLONIES
The red on this map shows where the Greeks settled around the edges of the seas. Settlers looked for a natural harbour, good soil and a climate similar to their homeland.

RICHES FROM THE COLONIES
This sceptre is covered in gold, wrapped in gold wire, and crowned with gold acanthus leaves. It was made in Taranto, a wealthy colony in southern Italy.

TIES WITH HOME
Settlers built new cities to look like those they had left behind. There was a central meeting place and a temple on the highest ground for their special god or goddess.

ON THE RUN
Nike was the winged goddess of victory. This bronze statue might once have adorned the rim of a bowl in southern Italy.

SAFE HARBOUR
Colonies were usually established beside the sea. Settlements developed their own systems of government but kept in touch with their homeland. Ships sailed to and fro carrying supplies and news.

THE ORACLE OF DELPHI

Leaders of colonising expeditions always consulted a priest in Apollo's temple at Delphi about where to settle. The buildings at the sacred site of Delphi on the steep slopes of Mount Parnassus were a centre of ancient Greek religious life. The vase below shows a procession on its way to visit Apollo's shrine. People believed Apollo answered questions about the future through his priestesses who spoke while in trances. Priests explained these answers, known as oracles. Oracles could often be understood in more than one way. So, whatever happened, the hearer would think that the oracle had come true.

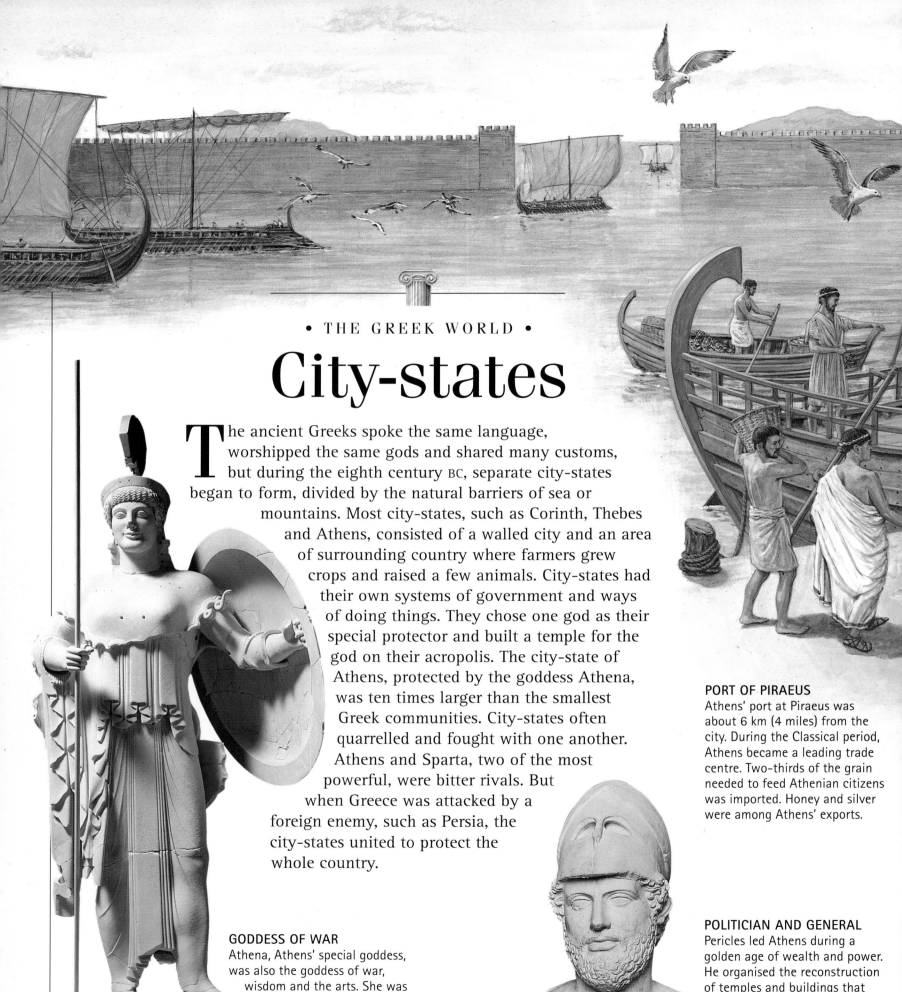

City-states

The ancient Greeks spoke the same language, worshipped the same gods and shared many customs, but during the eighth century BC, separate city-states began to form, divided by the natural barriers of sea or mountains. Most city-states, such as Corinth, Thebes and Athens, consisted of a walled city and an area of surrounding country where farmers grew crops and raised a few animals. City-states had their own systems of government and ways of doing things. They chose one god as their special protector and built a temple for the god on their acropolis. The city-state of Athens, protected by the goddess Athena, was ten times larger than the smallest Greek communities. City-states often quarrelled and fought with one another. Athens and Sparta, two of the most powerful, were bitter rivals. But when Greece was attacked by a foreign enemy, such as Persia, the city-states united to protect the whole country.

PORT OF PIRAEUS
Athens' port at Piraeus was about 6 km (4 miles) from the city. During the Classical period, Athens became a leading trade centre. Two-thirds of the grain needed to feed Athenian citizens was imported. Honey and silver were among Athens' exports.

GODDESS OF WAR
Athena, Athens' special goddess, was also the goddess of war, wisdom and the arts. She was said to have given Athens the first olive tree.

POLITICIAN AND GENERAL
Pericles led Athens during a golden age of wealth and power. He organised the reconstruction of temples and buildings that were destroyed when the Persians invaded Athens.

Discover more in Building in Stone

LIVING IN SPARTA

The city-state of Sparta was enclosed by a mountain range so it did not need protective walls. It was the only city-state to keep a permanent army, and Spartan soldiers were recognised as the best in ancient Greece. All Spartan children belonged to the state and boys began their tough military training at the age of seven. Even when they married, Spartan men still lived in army barracks.

TEST OF TIME
This painting from the nineteenth century shows how well some of the temples on Athens' acropolis survived through the centuries.

15

WATER CLOCK
In court, speakers were timed by a water clock. Their time was up when all the water from the upper pot had run into the lower one.

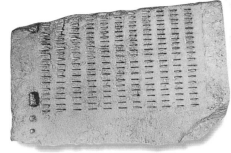

SELECTING A JURY
Citizens fitted their names into the slots of an allotment machine. A fragment of one is shown here. Coloured balls dropped beside the rows of names to show the jurors for that day.

• THE GREEK WORLD •

Government and the Law

In early times, groups of rich landowners ran the city-states, but sometimes one leader, called a tyrant, seized power. Tyrants usually ruled fairly, but some were cruel and unjust. Athens introduced a system of government called democracy. Many other city-states developed the same system. We know most about the way Athens was organised from surviving evidence. In Athens, democracy allowed every citizen to have a say in state affairs. But only men who were born in the city-state and were not slaves could become citizens. A council of 500 citizens, drawn annually in a lottery, suggested new laws and policies. Citizens voted at the assembly to accept, change or reject these suggestions. Juries of more than 200 citizens tried most Athenian law cases. Jurors were also chosen by lot. There were no lawyers, and only citizens could speak in court.

TRIAL BY JURY
After a trial, jury members cast their verdicts with bronze discs. They used tokens with solid centres to show the accused was innocent, and tokens with hollow centres to show the accused was guilty.

PUBLIC SPEAKER
Oratory is the art of making public speeches. Aeschines, the famous Athenian orator, started a school in Rhodes for speech makers.

POINTS OF VIEW
Any Athenian citizen, rich or
poor, could explain his point
of view to the assembly. At
least 6,000 citizens had to be
present before a meeting could
begin. Once all opinions about
a matter had been heard, the
whole assembly voted on it.

LOSING THE VOTE

The Athenians had a way of getting rid of
politicians they did not trust. Once a year,
assembly members could vote against the ones they
disliked. Citizens wrote the names of unpopular politicians
on pieces of pottery called ostraca. A man who received
more than 6,000 votes had to leave Athens for ten years. This
method of exiling people was called ostracism. Arissteides and
Kimon, named on these fragments, were both ostracised.

On Mount Olympus

The top of Mount Olympus, the highest mountain on mainland Greece, is often hidden by clouds. The ancient Greeks imagined that gods and goddesses, who looked and behaved like humans, lived on the mountain. However, these supernatural beings drank nectar and ate ambrosia, which made them immortal—they could not grow old or die. The people believed the gods and goddesses controlled events in life and nature, and had power to shape the future. Apollo made the sun rise and set. Hermes cared for travellers and led souls to the Underworld. Zeus, the king of the gods, roared with thunder and threw lightning bolts when he was angry. Poseidon whipped up storms at sea or caused earthquakes. Every village had its own guardian god or goddess although some were not important enough to live on Mount Olympus. The Greeks built temples for their deities and organised animal sacrifices, processions, plays and games to please them.

THINGS FROM THE PAST
Sometimes, archaeologists find it difficult to identify the things they find. This statue is thought to be the goddess Hera.

Head of Zeus

Zeus
God of the sky and thunder.

Poseidon
God of earthquakes, the sea, horses and bulls.

Hestia
Goddess of the family and the hearth.

Hermes
Messenger of the gods and protector of travellers.

Aphrodite
Goddess of love and beauty.

Athena
Goddess of wisdom, art and war.

Ares
God of war.

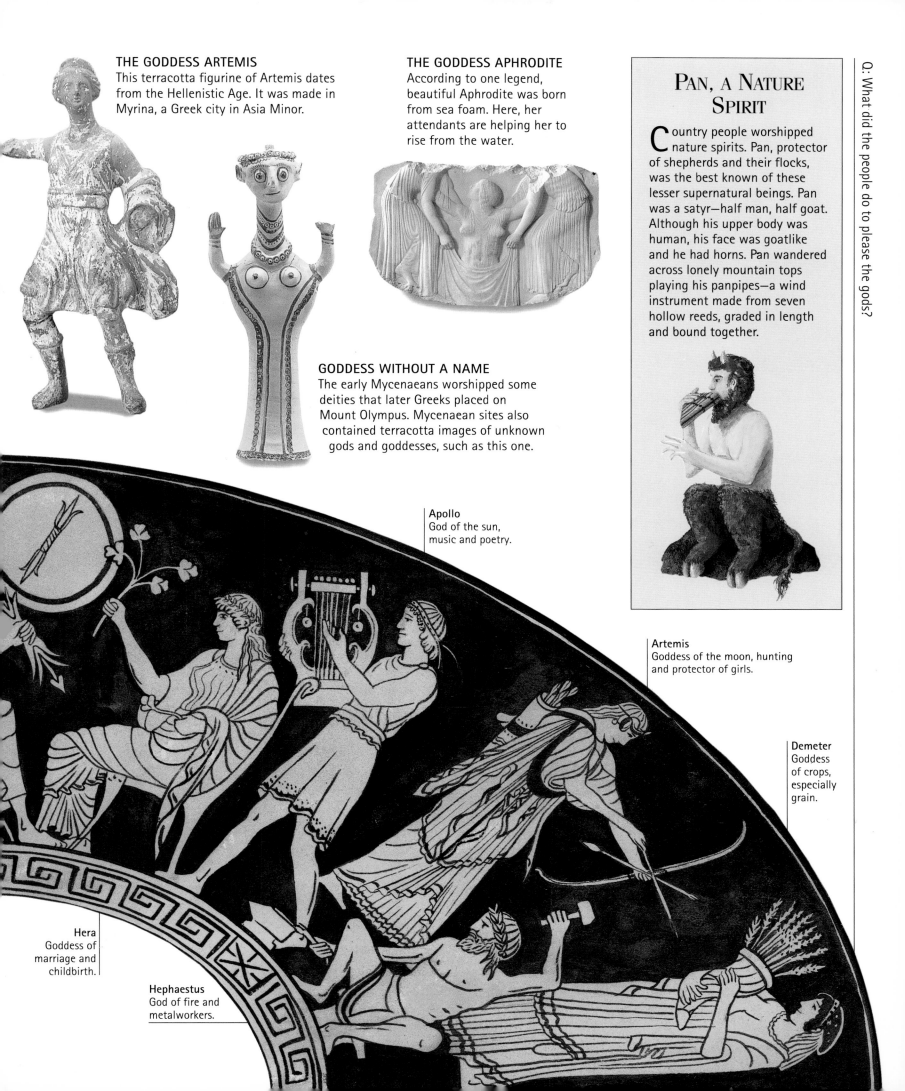

THE GODDESS ARTEMIS
This terracotta figurine of Artemis dates from the Hellenistic Age. It was made in Myrina, a Greek city in Asia Minor.

THE GODDESS APHRODITE
According to one legend, beautiful Aphrodite was born from sea foam. Here, her attendants are helping her to rise from the water.

GODDESS WITHOUT A NAME
The early Mycenaeans worshipped some deities that later Greeks placed on Mount Olympus. Mycenaean sites also contained terracotta images of unknown gods and goddesses, such as this one.

PAN, A NATURE SPIRIT

Country people worshipped nature spirits. Pan, protector of shepherds and their flocks, was the best known of these lesser supernatural beings. Pan was a satyr—half man, half goat. Although his upper body was human, his face was goatlike and he had horns. Pan wandered across lonely mountain tops playing his panpipes—a wind instrument made from seven hollow reeds, graded in length and bound together.

Apollo
God of the sun, music and poetry.

Artemis
Goddess of the moon, hunting and protector of girls.

Demeter
Goddess of crops, especially grain.

Hera
Goddess of marriage and childbirth.

Hephaestus
God of fire and metalworkers.

Stories of Daring Deeds

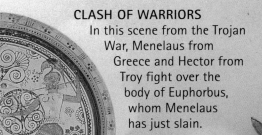

CLASH OF WARRIORS
In this scene from the Trojan War, Menelaus from Greece and Hector from Troy fight over the body of Euphorbus, whom Menelaus has just slain.

The heroes of Greek legends were usually successful in war or adventure. They inspired the ancient Greeks to be brave, strong and clever. Poets told stories about the heroes in long poems that people learnt by heart. Pottery, sculpture and other Greek art often showed heroic deeds. Heroes were helped by the gods and goddesses, and sometimes they even had an immortal as a parent. Zeus was the father of Heracles, the ancient Greek superman. Clothed in a lion's skin, Heracles faced great dangers. The story of the Trojan War had many heroes, such as the Greek warrior Achilles. Strange creatures in Greek mythology included Pegasus, the beautiful white-winged horse (above left), and the ugly Furies with dogs' heads, bats' wings and snakes for hair. Medusa, one of three hideous sisters, also had snakes for hair. Anyone who looked at her was turned to stone. The god Hermes showed Perseus, another son of Zeus, how to kill this monster.

GARDEN OF THE HESPERIDES
King Eurystheus ordered Heracles to steal the apples of eternal youth from a garden tended by nymphs called the Hesperides. A serpent with 100 heads guarded the apple tree. Heracles killed this monster and picked three golden apples. The gods made Heracles immortal for successfully completing the 12 tasks that Eurystheus had set him.

HALF MAN, HALF HORSE
Centaurs were shaped like a horse but had a man's head and upper body. Legend says that the healing god Asclepius learnt about medicine from a centaur.

THE 12 LABOURS OF HERACLES
Heracles, called Hercules in Roman myths, had to complete 12 difficult tasks for the legendary King Eurystheus. In one labour, Heracles had to fetch three-headed Cerberus from the Underworld.

THE WANDERINGS OF ODYSSEUS

Odysseus (called Ulysses in Roman mythology) was the king of Ithaca. He fought for ten years at Troy and took ten more years to sail home. On the way, he outwitted the one-eyed giant Cyclops, persuaded the enchantress Circe to help him, and visited the Underworld. Odysseus resisted the sirens who lured sailors to their death, and escaped from the sea nymph Calypso, pictured here. He eventually reached Ithaca, where his wife Penelope and son Telemachus were still waiting patiently for him to return.

DID YOU KNOW?
Greek myths sometimes told of living people visiting the Underworld. Heracles and Odysseus both went to Hades during their lifetimes and returned safely to Earth.

PAYING THE FERRYMAN
A coin, left with the dead person when he or she was buried, was later used to pay the fare to cross the River Styx. Without the fare, souls were lost. On the opposite bank, the fierce, three-headed dog Cerberus guarded the entrance to Hades.

OIL FOR THE DEAD
Women took offerings of perfumed oil to the tombs of their dead relatives. Tying ribbons around the tombstone was another way of showing respect for the dead.

WATER VESSEL
A jug, like this one depicting women in mourning, was placed on the tombs of people who died unmarried.

• THE GREEK WORLD •

Crossing the River Styx

When ancient Greeks died, they believed their souls travelled across the River Styx to the Underworld. This underground kingdom, called Hades, was ruled by the god Hades. A dead person lay at home for a day so that sad relatives and friends could say their farewells. Grieving women cut their hair short. The next morning, before dawn, a funeral procession took the body to the burial ground. There was music and weeping and wailing. Food, drink and personal belongings were placed in the tomb to give comfort in the afterlife. Once across the River Styx, which divided the living world from the Underworld, all souls faced three judges. Those who had been good on Earth were sent to everlasting happiness in the Elysian Fields. Wrongdoers had to endure endless punishments in Tartarus. Large crowds of souls who were neither good nor bad were condemned to wander forever on the dreary Plain of Asphodel.

FUNERAL PYRE
Human ashes found in graves from the Dark Age, and scenes on vases made much later, show that the Greeks cremated their dead as well as burying them.

A QUEEN FOR THE UNDERWORLD

Hades snatched Persephone, the beautiful daughter of the goddess Demeter, and made her his queen. Grief-stricken, Demeter forgot the crops and the harvest failed. People began to starve, and Zeus told Hades to release Persephone. Because Persephone could not stay on Earth if she had eaten in the Underworld, Hades tricked her into swallowing a pomegranate seed. Thereafter, Persephone was only allowed to spend two-thirds of the year above ground. When she returned to Hades, Demeter plunged the Earth into winter.

MYCENAEAN GRAVESTONE
Large stone slabs called stelae marked important people's graves. They were often elaborately carved. This one was found above a royal tomb in Mycenae.

Discover more in Going to War

CHILDREN'S TOYS
Spinning tops and dolls were made from terracotta—a mixture of clay and sand. The writing on the pottery baby's bottle says, "drink, don't drop!"

• LIVING IN ANCIENT GREECE •

In the Home

Houses had stone foundations, mud-brick walls and roofs of pottery tiles. Small, high windows kept out heat and burglars. Doors and shutters were made of wood. The central open courtyard contained an altar where the family worshipped their gods. Some courtyards also had a well, but water was usually fetched from public fountains. Women ran the household with the help of slaves. In ancient Greece, women had to obey their fathers, husbands, brothers or sons. A father could abandon his newborn child. He might do this if the baby was sickly, but healthy infant girls were also abandoned sometimes. Most women married at 15, while men married at 30 or more. The father chose his daughter's husband and gave the bridegroom money or valuables to save for his wife in case he wanted a divorce or died before she did. Sometimes, a bride met her husband for the first time on the day she was married.

WOMEN'S QUARTERS
Men and women had separate quarters. Women wove cloth in the loom room.

MEN'S QUARTERS
The head of the household entertained guests in a dining room furnished with couches.

LOOM DUTIES
The women of the family produced a great amount of cloth for household furnishings and clothing. Girls learnt how to spin and weave from their mothers.

GETTING MARRIED

On her wedding day, a bride bathed in sacred spring water and dressed in white. That night, the bridegroom and his friends came to fetch her. The very wealthy had horse-drawn chariots, while others had carts or walked. At the bridegroom's home, the couple knelt at the altar and his family showered them with nuts, dried fruit and sweets before they went to the bridal chamber. The next day, the two families celebrated at the husband's house.

DID YOU KNOW?

Children stopped being infants at the age of three. In Athens, at a spring festival, they were given miniature wine jugs, such as this, to mark the end of their babyhood.

IN THE KITCHEN
Slaves baked bread in a
pottery oven and cooked food on
an open fire. The smoke escaped
through a hole in the roof.

OUT TO PLAY
Girls played
knucklebones using
the ankle joints of
goats or sheep. But
the day before they
married, girls had
to leave all their
playthings at the
temple of Artemis.

HOME FURNISHINGS
Couches, tables, stools,
chairs, beds and storage chests
were made from wood and bronze.
Oil-burning lamps provided light. Wealthy
people had bathrooms in their homes and
plenty of slaves to fill the tubs with water.

Discover more in Eating and Drinking

• LIVING IN ANCIENT GREECE •

Writing and Education

Education in ancient Greece was not free. Only the sons of wealthy citizens could afford to go to school, where they attended classes from about the age of seven. The sons of poorer citizens learnt their father's trade. At 18, youths were trained to fight so they were prepared to go to war when necessary. Some girls were taught to read and write at home, but lessons in housework were considered much more important. One writer even said that sending a girl to school would be like "giving extra poison to a dangerous snake"! In Sparta, education was much tougher than elsewhere in Greece. When they were seven, Spartan boys went to board in army barracks. They were given so little to eat that they had to steal food. This was supposed to teach them to be cunning soldiers. Spartan girls attended gymnastics, dancing, music and singing lessons.

AT SCHOOL
Boys learnt reading, writing and arithmetic. Students wrote with pointed sticks on wooden tablets covered in soft wax. Mistakes could be rubbed out easily. Athletics and dancing were also important lessons.

INSPIRED BY MUSES
This stone carving shows three of the nine Muses, the goddesses of arts and science. They were thought to inspire poets, playwrights, musicians, dancers and astronomers.

GREEK ALPHABET
The word alphabet comes from two Greek letters—alpha and beta. There were 24 letters in the ancient Greek alphabet.

APOLLO AND THE MUSE
Apollo, god of music and poetry, is shown here talking to a Muse. Apollo worked closely with the nine goddesses.

THE DEVELOPMENT OF WRITING

The Linear B script on these clay tablets was adapted by the Mycenaeans from Minoan Linear A script. It was forgotten during the Dark Age. Greeks began to write again in the eighth century BC. They borrowed an alphabet from the Near Eastern Phoenicians and altered it slightly. Phoenicians wrote from right to left but the Greeks eventually reversed this direction. Early Greeks wrote only in capitals with no spaces between words and no punctuation.

MUSIC LESSON
Boys learnt to play the lyre and pipes from a teacher called a kitharistes. This teacher also taught poetry and students had to memorise very long poems.

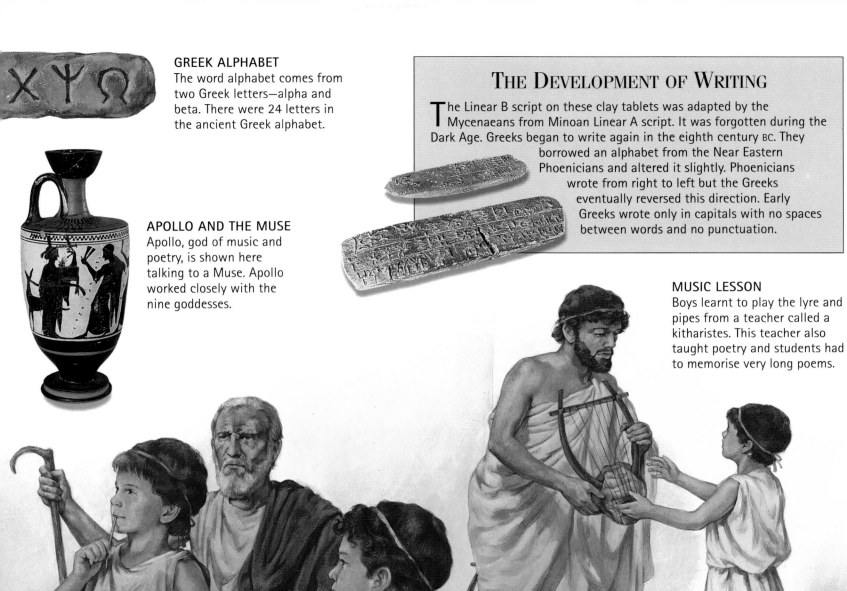

PIPES AND LYRES
Music lessons, like this one painted on a water vase, were often attended by several students. It seems that dogs and pet cheetahs were also welcome.

Discover more in Discovering Ancient Greece

Dressing for the Climate

Summers in ancient Greece were hot and dry. Winters were wet with chilly north winds. The poet Hesiod said that winter gales were cold enough to "skin an ox". People wore clothing made from rectangular pieces of material wrapped around the body in soft folds. They covered their summer garments with warm cloaks in winter. Statues and paintings on vases show that fashions changed slowly. The women of the household spun sheep's fleeces into fine woollen thread and flax fibres into linen. They dyed the yarns in bright colours and sometimes wove a contrasting colour or a pattern into the edge of the fabric. Imported silk cloth was very costly. Cotton was introduced into Greece after Alexander the Great reached India. The ancient Greeks went barefoot or wore sandals, shoes or boots. Wealthy men and women owned fine jewellery. Slaves in the mines and stone quarries, who were at the poorer end of the social scale, wore only loincloths.

DID YOU KNOW?

Suntans were unfashionable in ancient Greece. In summer, said Hesiod, "the sun scorches head and knees". Both men and women wore broad-brimmed hats to protect their faces when they went outdoors.

SHOULDER PINS
These bronze dress pins came from mainland Boeotia. They measure about 45 cm (18 in) in length.

MIRROR IMAGE
Containers of sweet-smelling oils often pictured lifelike figures on a background of white clay. Greek women cared greatly about face make-up and hairstyles.

WOMEN'S WEAR
Women wore a long tunic made of wool or linen, fastened on the shoulders with brooches or large pins and tied at the waist and sometimes at the hips. Wraps ranged from thin shawls to heavy travelling cloaks.

28

SPINNING AND WEAVING

Women and girls spent many hours weaving fabric from local sheep's wool. They made clothing for the household, wall hangings, and covers and cushions for wooden furniture. Raw wool had to be spun into thread before it could be woven into material. The woman pictured on the vase (left) is spinning with tools called a distaff and a spindle. In her left hand she holds the distaff wrapped in unspun wool. She pulls out the wool with her right hand and twists it slowly to form thread. The thread is fed onto the spindle, which is weighted to keep it steady.

JEWELLERY FROM RHODES
This chest ornament belonged to a rich man. He wore it by pinning the rosettes to his shoulders. The seven gold plaques show winged goddesses and lions. Pomegranates hang beneath them.

MENSWEAR
Men and boys usually wore thigh-length tunics; old men favoured longer hemlines. Winter cloaks were often draped to leave one shoulder bare.

ELEGANT FOLDS
Women wore two main tunic styles—folded over at the top (below left) and usually made from wool, or fastened on the shoulders in several places (below right) and usually made from linen.

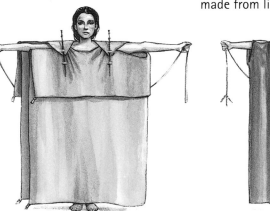

Discover more in Going to the Theatre

Making a Living

Many ancient Greeks worked hard. Fishermen and country folk provided food, such as sea creatures, olive oil, wine, grain, fruit, vegetables and honey, for people who lived in the towns. Farmers kept sheep, goats, pigs, poultry, donkeys and cattle, but only people in northern mainland Greece had enough pasture to breed horses. City people earned their living from making or selling things, such as leather goods, furniture, pots, tools, weapons and jewellery. It was unusual for well-born women to work outside the home, but some were priestesses in the temples. Low-born women became midwives, shopkeepers, dancers or musicians. Citizens who could afford to buy slaves or hire labourers looked down on those who had to work for a living. Rich men owned farms or ran silver mines and lived off the profits. They took part in public affairs, fought in the army when required, and paid high state taxes.

HARD AS IRON
During the Greek Dark Age, people learnt to forge iron. They began to make sickles and other farm tools out of this strong metal.

DAILY NEEDS
Women ground barley to make porridge, gruel and bread. They baked loaves in ovens. Wheat flour was more expensive and bought only by the wealthy.

METAL WORKING
Metal ores were heated in furnaces. Workers took the red-hot ore from the fire with tongs. They hammered it into shape while it was soft.

MAKING WINE

Grapes were picked when they ripened in September. A few bunches were set aside for eating. The rest were tipped into huge vats and stamped on to squeeze out the juice. This was poured into jars and left to ferment into wine.

SERVED BY SLAVES

Slaves did much of the work in ancient Greece. They were often prisoners of war or pirates' captives and were bought and sold in the markets. Many were educated. The children of slaves also became slaves. Sometimes slave traders reared abandoned babies to sell later. Household servants were usually treated well. A few even saved their tiny wages and bought their freedom. But slaves in the silver mines and stone quarries worked in terrible conditions.

OLIVE HARVEST

The scene on this vase shows men beating the ripe olives from the lower branches of olive trees with poles. Boys climbed the trees to reach the higher fruit.

Discover more in Sickness and Health

Meeting Place

LEAD WEIGHTS
Many things were sold by weight. In Athens, officials were chosen every year to inspect shopkeepers' weights. They checked that customers were not being cheated.

Every city had a central open space for meetings and markets. It was called the "agora". Men frequently did the shopping in ancient Greece and slaves carried the purchases. The agora must have been a noisy place, with customers jostling for attention at the covered stalls. Donkeys trotted to market bearing large loads of country produce. Strong smells mingled with fragrant, spicy odours. Merchants displayed foreign goods and stocked up with new cargoes to take to their next port. Some traders sold slaves and the poor offered themselves for hire as labourers. Citizens met friends under the shady colonnades to discuss business deals, politics and new ideas. Women came to fill their water pots. Altars and statues honouring gods, local athletes and politicians were erected in many marketplaces. The centre of Athens, surrounded by important government buildings, impressed all who visited the city.

DID YOU KNOW?
Sparta did not issue coins until three centuries after the other city-states. The Spartans used iron rods for money until the fourth century BC.

TEXTILE TRADE
The Athenians on this pot are hurrying across the agora with bales of cloth. Shops sold textiles made in foreign lands.

GOODS AND SERVICES
The marketplace provided all kinds of goods and services. Fishmongers sold fish, kept cool on marble slabs. Cobblers made sandals to fit the wearer's feet. Barbers trimmed hair and beards.

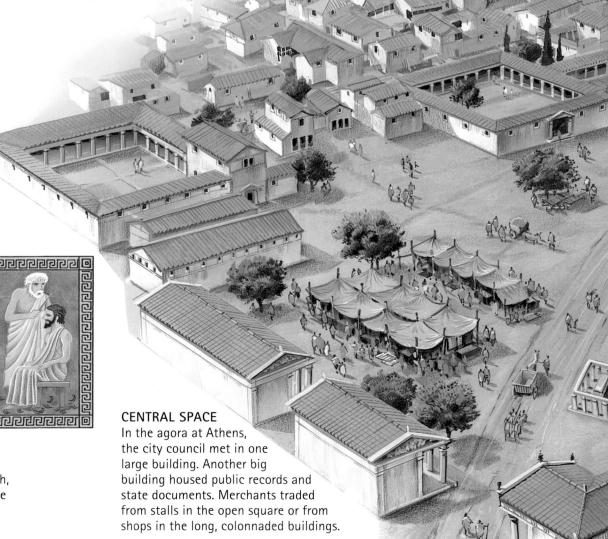

CENTRAL SPACE
In the agora at Athens, the city council met in one large building. Another big building housed public records and state documents. Merchants traded from stalls in the open square or from shops in the long, colonnaded buildings.

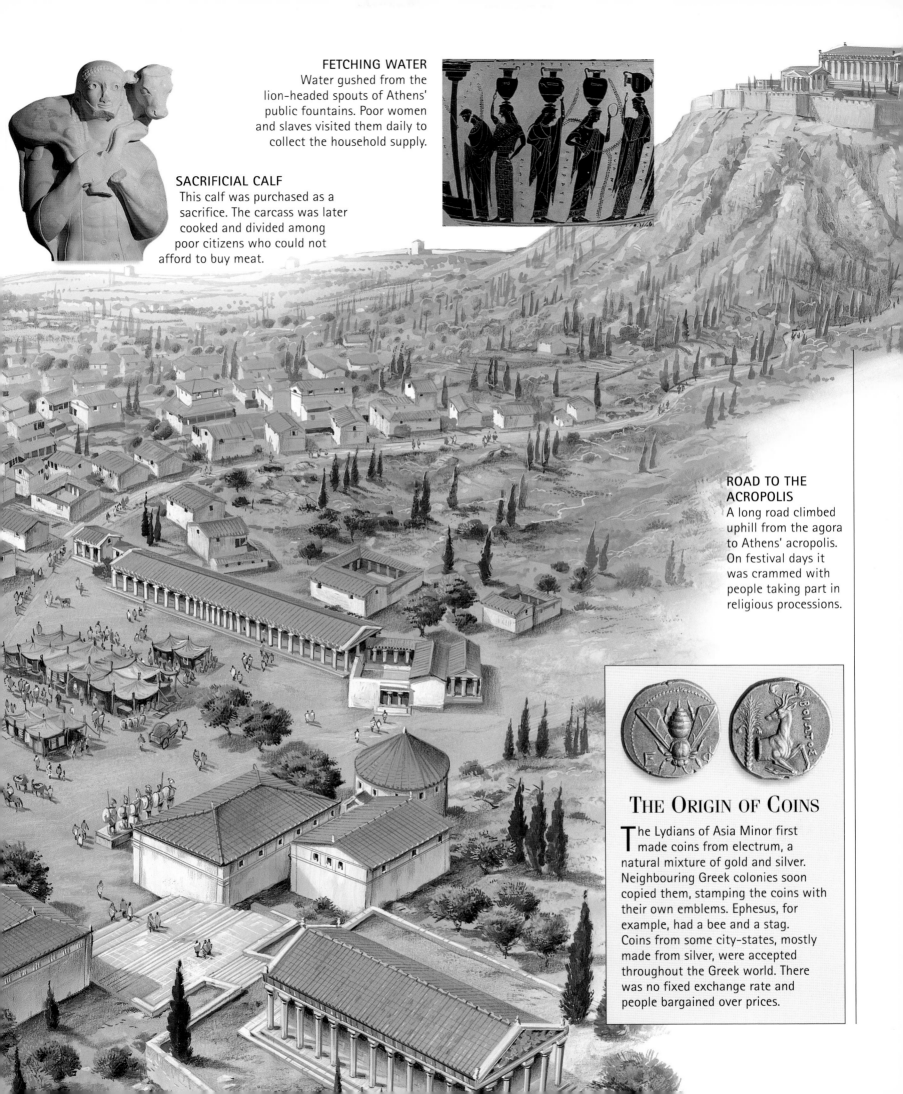

FETCHING WATER
Water gushed from the lion-headed spouts of Athens' public fountains. Poor women and slaves visited them daily to collect the household supply.

SACRIFICIAL CALF
This calf was purchased as a sacrifice. The carcass was later cooked and divided among poor citizens who could not afford to buy meat.

ROAD TO THE ACROPOLIS
A long road climbed uphill from the agora to Athens' acropolis. On festival days it was crammed with people taking part in religious processions.

THE ORIGIN OF COINS

The Lydians of Asia Minor first made coins from electrum, a natural mixture of gold and silver. Neighbouring Greek colonies soon copied them, stamping the coins with their own emblems. Ephesus, for example, had a bee and a stag. Coins from some city-states, mostly made from silver, were accepted throughout the Greek world. There was no fixed exchange rate and people bargained over prices.

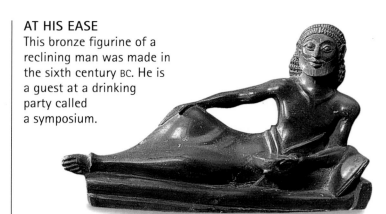

• LIVING IN ANCIENT GREECE •

Eating and Drinking

In early times, the Greeks worked extremely hard to produce enough food. They did not always succeed and there were famines during the Dark Age. Grape vines grew well on terraced hillsides and olive trees thrived in poor soil. But there was always the problem of needing more flat, fertile land for wheat and barley. Things improved once grain could be imported from the colonies or from Egypt. People ate greens—cabbage, lettuce, spinach and dandelion leaves—and root vegetables such as radishes, carrots and onions. Eggs, goat's milk cheese, almonds, figs and other fruit were also available. Squid, sea urchins, fish and shellfish were plentiful and provided protein. Meat was a rare treat reserved for the rich who could afford roast goat, sheep or pig, and for those who hunted wild deer, hares and boars. The Greeks sweetened their cakes and pastries with honey. Seasonings included garlic and herbs such as mint and marjoram.

STRINGED INSTRUMENTS
The kithara was a complicated form of lyre, usually played by professional musicians. They plucked the strings with a small instrument called a plectrum.

FEMALE COMPANIONS
Foreign or low-born women, called hetairai, amused the guests at symposiums. They were unmarried, beautiful, clever and trained in the art of conversation, making music and dancing.

MEN ONLY
Well-to-do Greek women did not attend symposiums, not even in their own homes. Slaves served the food and wine. Acrobats, jugglers and other professional performers provided entertainment.

DID YOU KNOW?

Greeks today use some vegetables that were unknown in ancient times. Peppers (capsicums), eggplants (aubergines), potatoes and tomatoes reached Europe in the 1500s, after the Spanish invasion of the Americas.

PARTY FOOD

At first, the food at symposiums was simple. By the third century BC, fashionable dinners began with roasted songbirds, artichoke hearts, mushrooms, grasshoppers, snails, fish roe and other snacks. Tuna fish, stuffed with herbs, might follow. Cooks often flavoured the meat course with cheese and aniseed, and the feast finished with honeyed sweetmeats, nuts and seeds. Bread was part of every meal. The Greeks used olive oil instead of butter.

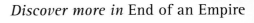

Discover more in End of an Empire

THE OLYMPIC OATH
During the Olympic ceremonies, a wild boar was sacrificed to Zeus. Athletes swore on this beast that they were freeborn Greeks and would not cheat.

TEST OF STRENGTH
The winner in upright wrestling had to throw an opponent three times and push the back of his shoulders to the ground.

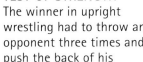

WOMEN'S GAMES
Women had their own games every four years to honour Hera, wife of Zeus. They ran foot races, which were divided into three different age groups.

FIRST PRIZE
Winners at the Panathenaic Games in Athens received jars of olive oil. The jar was decorated with a scene from the winner's sport.

DRESSED IN OIL
Athletes competed naked in all events except the chariot race. They oiled their body thoroughly beforehand and afterwards cleaned their skin with bronze scrapers.

DID YOU KNOW?
The modern Olympic Games introduced the marathon in memory of the soldier Pheidippides. In 490 BC, he ran about 35 km (22 miles) from the battlefield of Marathon to Athens.

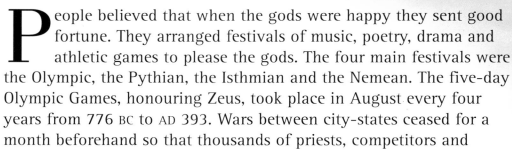

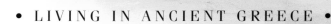

• LIVING IN ANCIENT GREECE •

Festival Games

People believed that when the gods were happy they sent good fortune. They arranged festivals of music, poetry, drama and athletic games to please the gods. The four main festivals were the Olympic, the Pythian, the Isthmian and the Nemean. The five-day Olympic Games, honouring Zeus, took place in August every four years from 776 BC to AD 393. Wars between city-states ceased for a month beforehand so that thousands of priests, competitors and spectators from all over Greece could travel to Olympia in peace. The valley looked like a huge fairground. The visitors put up tents and there were food stalls and entertainers. Women did not compete in the games, but unmarried women, foreigners and slaves could watch from the stadium. Ancient Olympic events included running, wrestling, boxing, and chariot and horse races. Jockeys rode bareback, and horses frequently finished without their riders!

OLYMPIC CONTESTS

The pentathlon tested all-round athletes in five skills. These were running, long jumping, wrestling, javelin throwing and discus throwing. The discus was a heavy circular plate of stone or bronze. The athlete rubbed it with sand for a good grip.

CROWNING THE WINNER

Athletes trained hard for the games. Winners received woolen ribbons, jars of olive oil, palm branches and wreaths. The crowning wreaths were made from olive leaves at the Olympics, laurel leaves at the Pythian Games, pine needles at the Isthmian Games and parsley sprigs at the Nemean Games. Crowds went wild when successful athletes returned home. Some city-states gave them presents and great banquets. Statues of sporting superstars (above) stood beside those of the gods in the temples and open spaces at Olympia.

Discover more in City-states

IN USE TODAY
At Epidaurus in the Peloponnese, plays are still performed at this theatre built in the 200s BC. Sound from the stage carries clearly to the back rows.

MASKED PERFORMERS

Actors performed wearing masks, modelled with detailed features made out of fabric stiffened with plaster. The large mouths helped carry the actor's voice to the back rows of the theatre. Each mask represented a person in the play and everyone in the enormous theatre recognised the characters as soon as they appeared. An actor changed his mask every time he played another role. There was a range of types of masks, for example, there were six varieties of young women. The mask's expression suggested what the character was feeling. Some masks had two faces. One side might show a calm expression while the other showed anger.

Terracotta copies of theatrical masks

Going to the Theatre

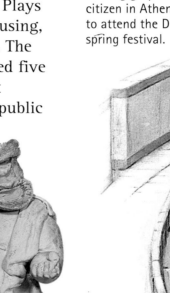

HONOURING DIONYSUS
The god Dionysus often appeared on Greek vases as a long-haired youth holding grapes or a wine cup. Every citizen in Athens was expected to attend the Dionysia spring festival.

Plays were first performed at festivals to honour the god Dionysus. In Athens, playwrights competed for prizes of ivy wreaths in competitions that were held twice a year. Plays called "tragedies" told stories of heroes and dealt with serious subjects such as obedience to the gods or using power wisely. Plays called "comedies" presented important citizens in amusing, unlikely situations and often made fun of the gods. The program began at daybreak and sometimes included five plays. Business stopped and prisoners were let out of jail for the day. The theatre was one of the few public places open to women. Audiences threw food or even stones at players who performed badly.

Actors, who were always men, wore masks (above left). Early plays had only one main actor and a "chorus" of 12 to 15 performers who danced and sang. Later plays had more parts that were divided between three leading actors. Aeschylus, Sophocles and Euripides wrote the best known Greek tragedies. Aristophanes wrote the most famous comedies.

COMIC ACTS
Actors in the chorus were skilled acrobats. They often performed energetically in the comic plays.

COMIC ROLE
A disobedient or runaway slave was often one of the characters in a Greek comedy. The playwright Aristophanes first created this role.

GOD OF WINE
Dionysus, god of the grapevine, was supposed to have inspired the great playwrights and to have given the gift of wine to Greece.

Thinking Things Through

BATHTUB DISCOVERY
One day Archimedes climbed into a full bathtub. As the water overflowed, he realised that the amount of water displaced by him was equal to the volume of his body. He shouted "Eureka", which means "I have found it", because this discovery helped him to work out how things float.

For centuries, ancient Greeks relied on myths and legends to explain natural events. But from about 600 BC onward, some people began to look for other ways to answer questions about the world. They were called philosophers, which means "lovers of knowledge". Other ancient peoples, such as the Egyptians, had to obey powerful rulers and could not express their own opinions safely. Greek citizens, however, were free to think for themselves and they discussed politics and philosophy openly. Some of the great Greek thinkers have inspired modern ideas. Socrates studied human behaviour; Plato considered the best way to govern a state; and Aristotle wrote about biology, zoology, physics, maths, astronomy, politics and poetry. Pythagoras identified a mathematical pattern in right-angled triangles. The theorem named after him is still taught in schools. Archimedes designed a screw-pump to clear water from ships. Pumps like this are used to irrigate crops in parts of Africa today.

ROSEMARY FOR REMEMBERING
Rosemary grows wild in Greece. In ancient times, students put sprigs of this herb in their hair while they were studying. They believed that rosemary had the power to strengthen their memories.

PASSING ON KNOWLEDGE
Plato (right) and Aristotle (left) were two of Greece's greatest philosophers. Plato learnt from Socrates. Aristotle studied at Plato's academy and later became Alexander the Great's tutor.

ARCHIMEDES' PUMP
This device consisted of a spiral screw inside a close-fitting covering. The turning screw forced water from a low level to a higher level.

MATHEMATICAL PATTERN
Pythagoras discovered that the square of the longest side (z) of a right-angled triangle is always equal to the sum of the squares of the other two sides (x and y).

THE LIFE AND DEATH OF SOCRATES

Socrates believed that it was important to develop a questioning mind. He made his students think carefully about human behaviour and examine the meaning of such things as truth, justice, courage, good and evil. Socrates' teaching alarmed some Athenians. Eventually he was sentenced to death for leading youth astray and disobeying religious laws. He died after drinking hemlock poison. Socrates wrote nothing himself, but Plato described his philosophies.

Sickness and Health

The ancient Greeks admired physical fitness. Citizens gathered at the public "gymnasium" to practise sports, bathe and discuss philosophy. Studies of skeletons show that many women died at about 35 years of age and men at about 44. According to written records, some philosophers lived very long lives. For centuries, ancient Greeks believed that the gods sent accidents and illnesses as punishments. Asclepius, the god of healing (above left), usually carried a snake coiled around his staff. Sick people made sacrifices at his temples, then stayed overnight, hoping to be cured as they slept. The temple priests were Greece's first doctors. They treated their patients with a mixture of magic and herbs, special diets, rest or exercise. Towards the end of the fifth century BC, Greek physicians, led by Hippocrates, began to develop more successful methods of healing. They tried to find out how the body worked and what caused diseases. They also noted the effects of different medicines.

JASON THE PHYSICIAN
A man's tombstone often showed what he did for a living. Here, an Athenian doctor called Jason examines a boy with a very swollen belly.

DOCTOR'S APPOINTMENT
From the time of Hippocrates onward, blood was thought to contain disease. Doctors sometimes removed a little from a patient's arm. Physicians prescribed herbal remedies for many complaints and consulted scrolls of recorded medical information.

Eyebright
The ancient Greeks soaked eyebright in hot water to make an eyewash.

Hyssop
Hippocrates prescribed hyssop for coughs, bronchitis and other chest infections.

Mullein
Mullein, also an ancient treatment for coughs, is still used today.

Motherwort
Motherwort was thought to ease the pain of heart disease and childbirth.

Smooth sow thistle
This oddly named herb was supposed to relieve stomach complaints and scorpion bites.

THE FATHER OF MEDICINE

Hippocrates, the founder of scientific medicine, practised and taught on the island of Cos. He said doctors could not understand the parts of the body until they understood the whole system. Hippocrates carefully observed patients' symptoms before making a diagnosis. In many countries, newly qualified doctors swear the Hippocratic oath, promising to care for the sick as well as they can.

SURGICAL INSTRUMENTS
Greek doctors did not perform many operations. Surgery, without anaesthetics and with simple instruments (right), was very painful. Patients often died from shock or infection.

DID YOU KNOW?

The ancient world had no protection against epidemic diseases. Between 430 and 429 BC, a terrible plague swept through Athens. The great Pericles was one of its victims.

WINE JUG

Some inventive potters began modelling parts of clay vessels. This jug, in the shape of a head, was made in the fourth century BC.

GIFTS FOR THE GODS

Small bronze horses, such as this mare with her foal, were made during the Geometric period. Worshippers left these statues in temples for the gods.

SHAPED IN TERRACOTTA

Many Greek cities produced terracotta figurines, each developing its own style. This sphinx, dating from the late fifth to early fourth century BC, came from southern Italy.

• ARTS AND SCIENCE •

Clay and Metal

The ancient Greeks loved beauty. They wanted buildings and useful objects to be balanced and graceful. Designers calculated how to fill spaces with the perfect amount of decoration. Early potters fashioned elegant vessels to be used as drinking cups, water jugs, storage jars for wine and olive oil, and for other practical purposes. From then onward, most potters used the same shapes. Large numbers of craftworkers made sandals, furniture, cooking vessels and other items for everyday use. In Athens, workshops lining the agora's south and west sides produced pottery, bronze and marble goods, and terracotta figurines. Athenian potters also lived and worked beside the cemetery. Metalworkers had quarters near the temple of Hephaestus—their special god. They used bronze for armour and household articles, and harder iron for tools and weapons that required sharp edges. Coins and jewellery were often made from gold and silver. Many craftworkers, especially those who produced weapons and armour, became very rich.

SILVER CHAIN

As the centuries passed, jewellers became more skilled at working silver and gold. This silver necklace was probably made in northern Greece between 420 and 400 BC.

DID YOU KNOW?

By the fifth century BC, 20,000 slaves were labouring in the silver mines near Athens. They worked shifts of ten hours in narrow tunnels lit by oil lamps.

POTTERY WORKSHOP

The use of the wheel gave potters both hands free to shape the clay. They prepared slip, a special liquid clay, for decoration and then fired the vessels in a kiln. Sometimes touches of colour were added to the pots after firing.

The Black and the Red

Thousands of pots survive from all over ancient Greece. From about 550 to 300 BC, Athenian "figure" ware was more popular than any other pottery. The vessels showed scenes from the lives of gods and heroes, as well as everyday subjects. Vase painters first developed the black-figure technique—drawing black figures on a red clay background (below left). Later, the red-figure technique (below right) became fashionable. Painters covered the red clay surface with a black slip background and left the figures outlined in red.

RUINS AT CORINTH
The temple of Apollo at Corinth was built of limestone in about 540 BC. At the time it was coated in white plaster to look like marble.

Building in Stone

Few houses or early public buildings of ancient Greece survive. They were made of timber and sun-dried mud bricks, and have crumbled and rotted away. Later structures of marble and limestone have survived earthquakes, fires, wars and weather. Throughout the Greek world, priests and priestesses cared for sacred sites. The best known site was the Acropolis, the hill overlooking Athens, where there was a collection of temples, altars, statues and memorial stones, as well as the state treasury. The Parthenon, a temple decorated with enormous sculptures, housed a statue of Athena. Pheidias, the sculptor in charge, made it from wood, gold and ivory. Like many other temples, the Parthenon was huge, rectangular in shape and surrounded by grooved (fluted) columns. The pieces of each column were heaved into place with winches and pulleys. Architects used clever tricks in their buildings such as making columns lean slightly inwards so that they would appear straight up and down from a distance.

PARTHENON RUINS
The Parthenon was built in Doric style between 447 and 432 BC. Plastic copies of the original marble-relief friezes are being used to restore the building.

HORSEMEN IN PROCESSION
A marble-relief frieze almost 160 m (525 ft) long ran like a ribbon under the roof around the Parthenon's four outer walls. It showed the Panathenaic festival procession.

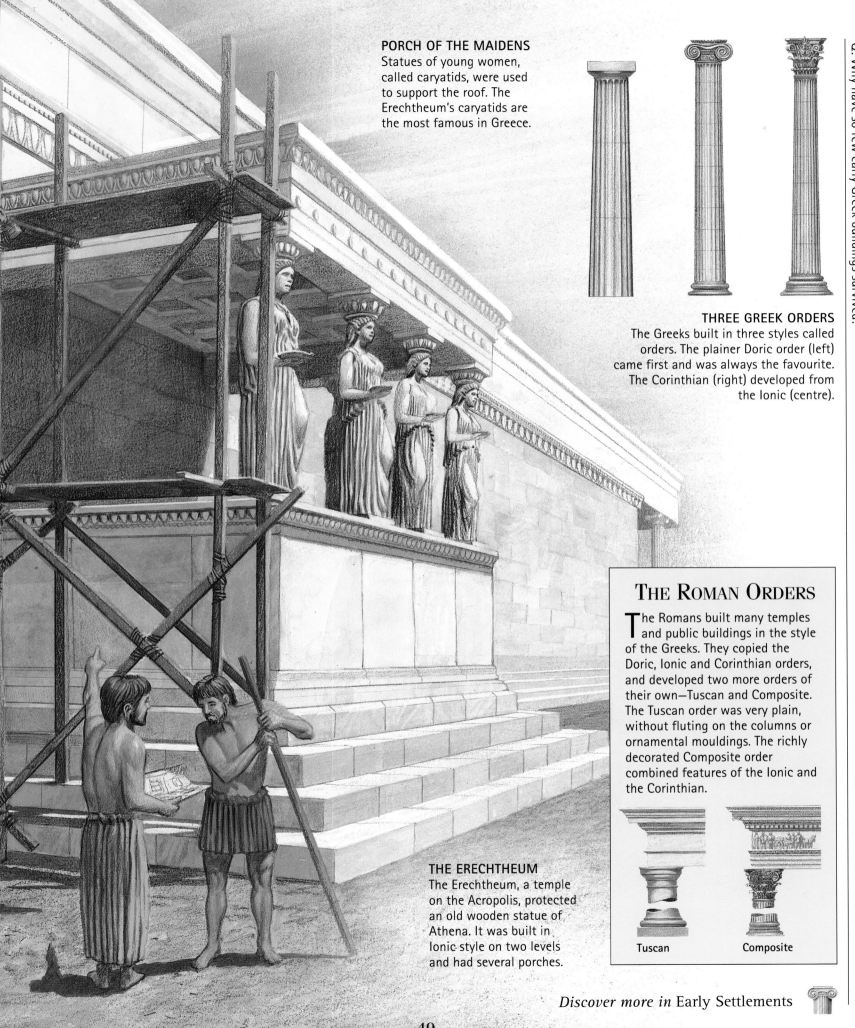

PORCH OF THE MAIDENS
Statues of young women, called caryatids, were used to support the roof. The Erechtheum's caryatids are the most famous in Greece.

THREE GREEK ORDERS
The Greeks built in three styles called orders. The plainer Doric order (left) came first and was always the favourite. The Corinthian (right) developed from the Ionic (centre).

THE ROMAN ORDERS

The Romans built many temples and public buildings in the style of the Greeks. They copied the Doric, Ionic and Corinthian orders, and developed two more orders of their own—Tuscan and Composite. The Tuscan order was very plain, without fluting on the columns or ornamental mouldings. The richly decorated Composite order combined features of the Ionic and the Corinthian.

Tuscan   Composite

THE ERECHTHEUM
The Erechtheum, a temple on the Acropolis, protected an old wooden statue of Athena. It was built in Ionic style on two levels and had several porches.

Discover more in Early Settlements

49

Going to War

The ancient Greek city-states fought each other over land and trade. Sparta had a full-time army, but other city-states trained freeborn men to fight and called them up in times of war. In Athens, men aged between 20 and 50 had to defend their state whenever necessary. Greeks who could afford horses usually joined the cavalry, but most served as foot soldiers called hoplites. Poorer citizens who were unable to buy their own weapons and armour rowed the warships. When the Persians invaded Greece, some city-states banded together against the foreigners. The Persian Wars lasted from 490 to 449 BC, and in 480 BC the Persian army destroyed Athens. In 447 BC the Greeks rebuilt the city. Sparta fought Athens for 27 years in the Peloponnesian War from 431 to 404 BC. Both sides were supported by other city-states. Sparta eventually won, but every city-state that took part in the conflict was weakened by loss of lives and money.

BATTLE SCENES
War was a common theme in vase art. These paintings provide useful information about the way warriors dressed for battle and the weapons they used.

DID YOU KNOW?
The Athenian navy had long, narrow, timber warships called triremes. In battle, a trireme was powered by 170 oarsmen. They tried to sink enemy ships by ramming them with the bronze prow.

BODY SHIELDS

Hoplites carried shields, made of bronze or leather, to protect them from neck to thigh. The symbols on the soldiers' shields represented their family or city.

FIGHTING THE AMAZONS

The Amazons were legendary women warriors who were believed to have helped Troy in the Trojan War. This marble frieze shows the Greeks and Amazons fighting.

PROTECTIVE CLOTHING

Soldiers wore bronze or leather breast and back plates joined on the shoulders and at the sides. Helmets, which came in various styles, protected their head and face.

FIRST HISTORIANS

Herodotus, who wrote a history of the Persian Wars, has been called the father of history. He travelled widely to get information for his books. Another ancient Greek called Thucydides wrote a history of the Peloponnesian War. Both Herodotus and Thucydides tried to write factual accounts of what had happened. They interviewed many people who had fought in the wars.

Q: What did a Greek hoplite wear to battle?

VICTORY AT SEA

After the Persians destroyed Athens, the Greek fleet trapped the Persian fleet in a narrow channel of water between the island of Salamis and the Greek mainland. There, the Greek triremes rammed the larger Persian warships and forced them to retreat.

COURAGEOUS LEADER
Alexander the Great was a fearless soldier and was often wounded. This mosaic shows him riding, without a helmet, into the thick of the Battle of Issus against King Darius of Persia.

MACEDONIAN MEDALLIONS
These medallions were found in Egypt. The one on the left shows Philip II with his attendants. The other portrays Alexander.

• FOREIGN AFFAIRS •

The Macedonians

Macedonia in northeastern Greece was not a democratic city-state. It was ruled by kings who claimed to be descended from Macedon, a son of Zeus. For centuries, Macedonia was weak and frequently overrun by invaders. When Philip II came to power, he began to improve Macedonia's fortunes. By 338 BC, he controlled all of Greece and afterwards declared war on Persia. When Philip II was murdered in 336 BC, he was succeeded by his 20-year-old son Alexander, who eventually conquered Persia in 333 BC. Alexander (left) had blond hair and eyes of different colours—grey-blue and dark brown. He loved reading the *Iliad* and modelled himself on two great heroes, Achilles and Heracles. Alexander fought many successful battles and seized kingdoms throughout the eastern world. He earned the title "the Great" and married a Persian princess. When he died in 323 BC, his vast empire stretched as far as India.

HUNTING FOR SPORT
Alexander, whether hunting or fighting, was a popular subject with sculptors. This is part of a carving on the tomb of a king of Sidon in ancient Phoenicia.

ON THE MOVE
The Macedonian army trudged long distances through deserts and over mountains. Besides thousands of cavalry and foot soldiers, there were servants, grooms, women, children, pack animals and wagons. Indian elephants became part of the Macedonian army after Alexander's death.

52

FIGHTING IN FORMATION

Philip II trained his hoplites to fight in a formation called a phalanx. In battle, the front ranks extended their long spears. The men behind rested their spears on the row in front to form a barrier against arrows. A phalanx's weakest point was the right side where the men were only half protected by their shields. Flute music helped the marching hoplites to stay in step.

DID YOU KNOW?

When Alexander was eight or nine, he tamed a pedigree stallion that had defeated his father's horse trainers. Alexander rode this horse, Bucephalus, into almost all his major battles.

The Hellenistic World

The ancient Greeks called their country "Hellas" and themselves "Hellenes". After Alexander the Great died, the three generals Antigonus, Seleucus and Ptolemy divided up his empire between them. Antigonus ruled Macedonia and the rest of Greece and founded the Antigonid royal family. Seleucus took Asia Minor, Persia, and other eastern countries and began the Seleucid line of rulers. Ptolemy governed Egypt as the first ruler of the Ptolemaic dynasty. This was the beginning of the Hellenistic Age when Greek customs and ideas spread far beyond the boundaries of Greece. Architects building new cities throughout the Hellenistic world used Greek styles. These settlements adopted Greek law and language and the people attended Greek entertainment in theatres and stadiums. Hellenistic artists were interested in realism. Portraits on coins throughout the empire began to represent people's faces rather than making everyone look like gods or heroes. Sculptors chose a wider range of subjects and showed childhood, old age and suffering in a realistic way.

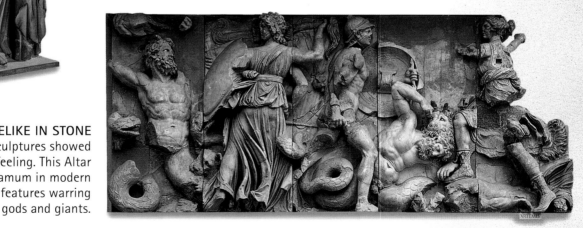

LIFELIKE IN STONE
Hellenistic sculptures showed movement and feeling. This Altar of Zeus at Pergamum in modern Turkey features warring gods and giants.

THE PTOLEMIES OF EGYPT

The Ptolemy dynasty governed Egypt from 323 to 30 BC. In Alexandria, Ptolemy I (left) built a huge library that had laboratories, observatories and a zoo. This city soon became the most important centre of learning in the ancient world. The Ptolemy dynasty taught the Egyptians many Greek ways, but Cleopatra VII, the last ruler of the dynasty, was the only one who spoke Egyptian as well as Greek. After her death, the Romans took over Egypt.

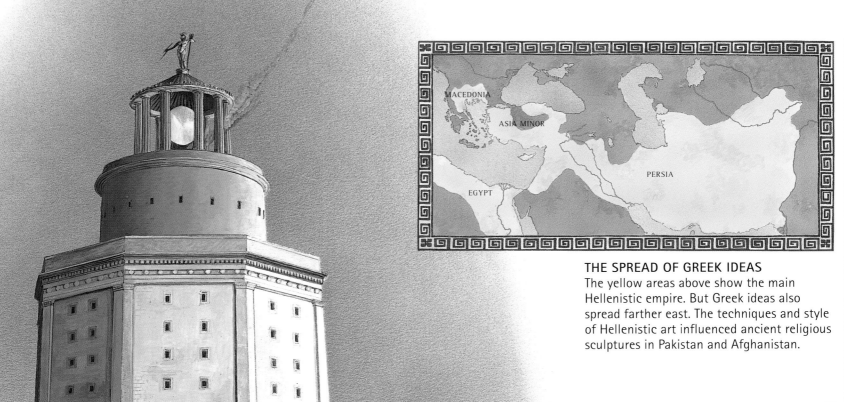

THE SPREAD OF GREEK IDEAS

The yellow areas above show the main Hellenistic empire. But Greek ideas also spread farther east. The techniques and style of Hellenistic art influenced ancient religious sculptures in Pakistan and Afghanistan.

THE FACE OF MEDUSA

This Hellenistic statue of Medusa, one of the hideous Gorgons, adorns a temple in Turkey. Her features, especially the dimpled chin, are more human-looking than earlier statues. Ringlets replace the snaky hair.

ALEXANDRIA

Alexander the Great set up many new cities called Alexandria. The first one, where he was later buried, was in Egypt. A three-tiered lighthouse was built in the harbour. The light from the fire at the base was reflected by a series of bronze mirrors and could be seen far out at sea.

TWO NAMES—ONE GOD
The Romans renamed most of the Greek gods and heroes when they adopted Greek mythology as their own. Hephaestus, the Greek god of fire, became Vulcan.

VULCAN. [1032]

• FOREIGN AFFAIRS •

End of an Empire

The division of Alexander the Great's empire by his generals weakened Greece's hold on the ancient world. From 509 BC, a new power—Rome—had been growing in Italy. Roman rule spread gradually across the Hellenistic world. In 275 BC, the Romans captured the Greek colonies in southern Italy and Sicily. Between 148 and 146 BC, Macedonia and all of southern Greece became part of the Roman Empire. To the east, the Hellenistic empire slipped away as Rome acquired one kingdom after another. Finally, the Roman emperor Augustus defeated the Egyptians in 31 BC and demanded Cleopatra VII's surrender. The following year Cleopatra killed herself and Egypt became the last province in the Greek empire to fall into Roman hands. Although Greece no longer existed as a political and military power, Greek literature, art and architecture became models for the Romans who also adopted Greek gods and heroes. Many Roman boys were educated in Athens before Athenian schools closed down in the sixth century AD.

GODDESS JUNO
This Roman bust of Juno, wife of Jupiter, was copied from a Greek original. In Greek mythology, Juno and Jupiter were known as Hera and Zeus.

TRAVELLING TREASURES

The Romans admired and valued Greek sculpture and other works of art. They stole many treasures on their journey of conquest through the Greek city-states. Roman generals organised triumphant processions to carry the treasures through the streets of Rome.

THE GREEK ORTHODOX CHURCH

Byzantium was a Greek colony from mid-600 BC until the Romans occupied it in mid-100 BC. The Roman emperor Constantine renamed the city Constantinople. This city became the centre of eastern Christendom and Christians living there founded the Greek Orthodox Church. Religious pictures, called icons (above), are sacred to Greek Orthodox worshippers. Early religious artists used ancient Greek styles. Constantinople is now Istanbul, the capital of Turkey.

TEMPLE OF ZEUS

The Roman architect Cossutius began the temple of Zeus in Athens in 174 BC. This Corinthian-style building, which took until AD 132 to finish, was the largest Hellenistic shrine on mainland Greece.

PORTRAIT ON WOOD

Like the Egyptians, Roman citizens living in Egypt mummified their dead. Roman artists copied Greek styles and painted lifelike portraits, such as this, on the mummy cases.

Discover more in Writing and Education

• FOREIGN AFFAIRS •

Discovering Ancient Greece

SHIPWRECKED EROS
This bronze statue of Eros was found off the coast of Tunisia in modern times. It was part of a cargo of Greek art bound for ancient Roman villas in North Africa.

When Pericles planned to rebuild Athens in the fifth century BC, he said, "Future ages will wonder at us, as the present age wonders at us now". His words have come true, for people still admire ancient Greece. They can study Greek art and architecture and visit museums to see what has been collected from ancient sites. Archaeologists continue their quest for information about ancient Greece. Clues about Greek civilisation are still being found in shipwrecks as well as from beneath the ground. By the 1980s, experts knew enough about triremes to build one and sail it on the Aegean Sea. Most Greek writing is lost forever, but some stone inscriptions and copies of manuscripts survive, and we can still learn to speak and write ancient Greek. Echoes of ancient Greece also linger in languages and systems of government. Perhaps you live in a democracy or speak words that come from ancient Greek such as "theatre", "orchestra", "gymnasium" and "Olympic".

ARCHITECTURE LIVES ON
Since the eighteenth century, architects designing public buildings have often used Greek styles. The front porch of this bank in Philadelphia, the United States, has Greek columns.

IN THE BRITISH MUSEUM
Part of the Parthenon was destroyed in 1687 when gunpowder accidentally exploded. Lord Elgin, an art collector, later bought some of the damaged sculptures for Britain.

CLUES FROM THE SEA

The ancient Greeks made hazardous sea voyages, with few navigational aids. Many ships sank. With the help of modern scientific equipment, divers can find some of these shipwrecks and retrieve cargoes that have lain undisturbed for centuries under the water.

Q: Why were so many ships wrecked in ancient Greek times?

THE RENAISSANCE

The Renaissance was a period in history that began in Italy in the fourteenth century AD and spread throughout Europe. During this time, writers, sculptors, architects and painters rediscovered ancient Greek artists and scholars and turned to them for inspiration. This Renaissance painting by Alessandro Allori shows the sea nymph Ino rescuing Odysseus after he was shipwrecked. The great Italian Renaissance artists Michelangelo, Raphael and Leonardo da Vinci were influenced by Greek art.

DID YOU KNOW?

In shipwrecks divers have found pottery jars that once held olive oil or wine. One sunken cargo included the remains of more than 10,000 almonds, probably grown on the island of Cyprus.

Portraits from Ancient Greece

Greek art from the Bronze Age onward portrayed gods, heroes and important people. They were featured on wall and vase paintings and in sculpture. Statues adorned temples and homes, marked graves, and were erected in public places. Few of the early statues made from wood survive, but many portraits in clay, stone and bronze have lasted. Although the bigger bronze figures were often melted down so that the metal could be reused, some large bronze statues have been recovered from shipwrecks.

Late Bronze Age
1600–1100 BC

MYCENAEAN SCULPTURE
This painted plaster statue was found on the acropolis at Mycenae. The artist has highlighted the cheeks and chin of this woman who is a goddess or a sphinx.

BRONZE AGE
3200–1100 BC

Early Bronze Age
3200–2000 BC

SCULPTURE FROM THE CYCLADES
Many marble figures, carved in the same style as this one, were made on the Cyclades islands in the early Bronze Age. Here, a musician is plucking a harplike instrument.

DARK AGE AND GEOMETRIC PERIOD
1100–700 BC

PATTERNED CENTAUR
Few works of art survive from the centuries known as the Dark Age, when it seems the Greeks had to struggle just to stay alive. This pottery centaur displays strong geometric patterns.

Middle Bronze Age
2000–1600 BC

MASTER OF THE ANIMALS
Figures appeared in Minoan jewellery made between 1700 and 1500 BC. This intricate golden pendant shows a Cretan god clasping two geese by their necks. His feet are shown pointing the same way.

FIGURES IN SILHOUETTE
During the last century of the Dark Age, human figures were painted within the patterned bands on pots. They were shown in silhouette and, like these, were often taking part in a funeral.

ARCHAIC PERIOD
700–480 BC

EGYPTIAN INFLUENCE
In the Archaic period, sculptors began making statues of young men and women from stone or bronze. Archaic artists learnt figure sculpture from the Egyptians, but used more relaxed poses.

CLASSICAL PERIOD
480–323 BC

PARTHENON SCULPTURE
By Classical times, figures such as this one of Dionysus or Heracles had become more like real human beings. The sculptor Pheidias designed the sculptures that decorated the Parthenon, but he did not carve them all.

HEAD OF APOLLO
Classical sculptors modelled faces in a more lifelike way, but they still did not make them completely realistic. This is one of the few surviving bronze sculptures from this period.

HELLENISTIC AGE
323–31 BC

VENUS DE MILO
Hellenistic sculptors portrayed the human form and clothing with great realism and attention to detail. This statue of Aphrodite (Venus) was found on the island of Milos in the Cyclades.

PREPARING TO KILL
Many Hellenistic statues showed people's actions and feelings at dramatic moments. In this one, cast in bronze in about 100 BC, a young hunter tenses his body before he spears an animal.

Glossary

Rosemary

Mycenaean fresco

Miniature wine jug

Voting tokens

Terracotta statue

acropolis Meaning "high city". In Mycenaean times most of a city was on high ground. Later, Greeks placed temples and shrines and other important buildings on hills above their cities.

AD An abbreviation for the Latin *anno Domini*, meaning "in the year of our Lord". Used for the measurement of time, AD indicates the number of years since the supposed date of Christ's birth.

Aeschines (c.389–c.322 BC) A soldier, actor and clerk who later became one of the most famous orators in Athens.

Aeschylus (c.525–c.456 BC) Regarded as the founder of Greek tragedy. He wrote about 60 plays. Seven of them survive.

agora The open space in the middle of a Greek city used for meetings and markets.

ambrosia The food of the gods that made them immortal and prevented them from growing old.

archaeologist A person who describes the way people lived by studying the things they left behind, such as buildings, tools and weapons.

Archimedes (c.287–c.212 BC) A mathematician, inventor and engineer. He studied in Alexandria, Egypt. He was murdered by a Roman soldier at his home in Syracuse.

architecture The art of planning, designing and constructing buildings.

Aristophanes (c.448–c.380 BC) A playwright who made fun of the political situations of his day. He is said to have written 54 comedies, but only 11 survive.

Aristotle (c.384–c.322 BC) A philosopher, scientist and writer. Aristotle is one of the most important people in the history of Western thought.

assembly The main governing body of a democratic city-state. All citizens had the right to attend the assembly.

BC Before Christ. Used for the measurement of time, BC indicates the number of years before the supposed date of Christ's birth.

black-figure ware A style of decorating pottery that featured black figures on a red background.

bronze A combination of copper and tin. In ancient Greece, lead was sometimes added.

Bronze Age The period of time when a civilisation first discovered how to make bronze and then used it for tools, weapons and other things.

c. An abbreviation of *circa,* which means "about". Used with dates to mean "at the approximate time of".

caryatid A column carved in the shape of a young woman.

centaur A mythical being half man, half horse.

century A period of time lasting 100 years.

citizen A freeborn Greek man entitled to take part in the government of his city-state.

civilisation An organised society that has developed social customs, government, technology and the arts.

colonnade A set of evenly spaced columns that support a roof.

Corinthian column A grooved pillar, built of sections of stone, used in the Corinthian order. The top was decorated with carved acanthus leaves.

democracy In ancient Greece, a system of government in which all citizens could have a say.

Doric column A grooved pillar with a plain top, built of sections of stone, used in the Doric order.

electrum A mixture of gold and silver. This occurred naturally in Asia Minor and was made into coins throughout ancient Greece.

emery A hard, greyish-black rock used for smoothing and polishing.

Euripides (c.480–c.406 BC) A writer of tragedies. He wrote between 80 and 90 plays, but only 18 complete ones survive.

fresco A painting made with watercolours on wet plaster.

frieze A strip of painting or carving that often tells a story.

Herodotus (c.485–c.425 BC) A writer who is regarded as the father of history. He based his reports of the Persian Wars on eyewitness accounts and facts.

Hesiod (8th century BC) One of ancient Greece's earliest poets. He owned a farm in Boeotia.

Hippocrates (c.460–c.377 BC) A doctor, teacher and writer on medicine who is regarded as the father of medicine.

Homer (8th century BC) A poet who recited his long story poems, which were called epics. Very little is known about him except that he is thought to have been blind.

Iliad Homer's long story poem about the war between the Greeks and the Trojans that was said to have lasted ten years.

Ionic column A grooved pillar, built of sections of stone, used in the Ionic order. It was taller and more slender than the Doric column. The top was decorated with two swirls called volutes.

Linear A An early form of writing used by the Minoans.

Linear B A form of writing that the Mycenaeans adapted from Linear A.

loom A wooden frame used to hold the threads during the process of weaving.

Lydia A small, but wealthy state in Asia Minor.

mosaic A pattern or a picture made from tiny pieces of coloured stone or glazed earthenware.

nectar The drink of the gods.

nymph A spirit of nature in Greek myth.

Odyssey Homer's long story poem about the adventures of the Greek hero Odysseus.

oracle A message spoken by a priest or priestess on behalf of a god.

order A style of architecture. The three Greek orders were Doric, Ionic and Corinthian.

Pericles (c.490–c.429 BC) An Athenian statesman and general. He was also a powerful public speaker who influenced people's opinions.

Pheidias (5th century BC) Considered to be the greatest sculptor in ancient Greece. Pericles asked Pheidias to design the sculptures for the Parthenon and the statue of Athena.

philosopher A person who searches for knowledge and wisdom. Ancient Greek philosophers studied the natural world and human behaviour. Some of their writings survive.

Plato (c.427–c.347 BC) An Athenian philosopher. Plato's ideas for running an ideal state are still studied today.

porch The covered entrance to a temple or other large building with its roof supported by columns.

prow The front part, or bow, of a boat.

pumice A volcanic stone used for polishing marble and other hard stone.

Pythagoras (c.580–c.500 BC) A philosopher, mathematician and teacher. Pythagoras developed many theories of geometry.

red-figure ware A style of decorating pottery that featured red figures on a black background.

relief A shallow carving on a flat slab of stone.

satyr A mythical being half man, half goat.

Schliemann, Heinrich (1822–1890) A German archaeologist. At 46, he began devoting his time to excavating the sites of Mycenae and Troy.

shrine A place where the ancient Greeks worshipped one of their gods.

slip Liquid clay, the thickness of cream, used for painting backgrounds on vases.

Socrates (c.470–c.399 BC) An Athenian philosopher. He taught his students by questions and answers and encouraged them to discuss weaknesses in the government and people's beliefs.

Sophocles (c.496–c.406 BC) An Athenian playwright who wrote more than 100 works for the theatre. Seven of his tragedies survive.

sphinx A mythical creature usually depicted with the head of a woman and the body of a lion.

terracotta Unglazed clay used to make tiles and for modelling small statues.

Thucydides (c.460–c.395 BC) An Athenian historian who wrote an account of the Peloponnesian War.

trance A hypnotic state resembling sleep. At Greek shrines, priests and priestesses often fell into a trance before speaking oracles.

trireme A Greek warship with three rows of oars.

Roman god Vulcan

Theatrical mask

Minoan double axe

Discus

Archimedes' screw

Index

A

Achilles, 20, 52
acropolis, 10, 14, 15, 33, 60, 62
Acropolis, 48
actors, 39–40, 42
Aeschines, 16, 62
Aeschylus, 39, 62
Agamemnon, King, 10
agoras, 32–3, 46, 62
agriculture, 8, 10, 12, 14, 30, 34
Alexander the Great, 28, 38, 52, 53, 54, 56
Alexandria, 54–5
alphabet, 26–7
animals, 8, 11, 18, 30, 33, 36, 44
Antigonas, 54
Aphrodite, 10, 18, 19, 54, 61
Apollo, 13, 18, 19, 27, 48, 61
archaeology, 8, 18, 58–9, 62
Archaic period, 7, 61
Archimedes, 38, 43, 62
architecture, 24–5, 48–9, 56, 58
Ares, 18
Arissteides, 17
Aristophanes, 39, 62
Aristotle, 38, 62
armed forces, 15, 26, 30, 50–3
armour, 9, 10, 50, 51, 53
Artemis, 19, 25
arts, 7, 8–9, 34–5, 39–42, 46–9, 54, 56, 58, 60–1
Asclepius, 20, 44
Asia Minor, 10,12, 33, 54
assemblies, 16–17, 62
Athena, 14, 18, 48, 54
Athens, 14, 15, 16, 17, 32–3, 39, 45, 46, 48, 50, 56, 57, 58
athletics, 26, 36–7, 44

B–C

black-figure ware, 47, 62
boys, 26, 29
bronze, 6, 12, 46, 51, 60, 62
Bronze Age, 6, 34, 60, 62
buildings, 24–5, 48–9, 54–5
Byzantium, 57
cavalry, 50, 52
centaurs, 20, 60, 62
Cerberus, 20, 22
children, 15, 24, 25, 26–7
Christianity, 57
citizenship, 16, 17, 30, 32, 50, 62
city-states, 14–15, 50, 62

Classical period, 7, 61
Cleopatra VII, 54, 56
clothing, 24, 28–9, 51
coins, 12, 32, 33, 46, 54
colonies, 12–13, 34, 54–7
columns, 48–9, 58
comedies, 39
Composite order, 49
Constantine, 57
Constantinople, 57
Corinth, 14, 48
Corinthian order, 49, 57, 62
Cossutius, 57
craftworkers, 30, 32, 46–7
Crete, 6, 8, 9
Cycladic civilisation, 6, 7, 8, 60
Cyclops, 21
Cyprus, 10

D–F

dance, 26, 30, 34–5, 39
Dark Age, 7, 12, 34, 60
death, 22–3, 57
Delphi, 13
Demeter, 19, 23
democracy, 16, 62
Dionysus, 39, 61
doctors, 44–5
Doric order, 48, 49, 62
drama, 36, 39–42
eating and drinking, 22, 34–5
education, 26–7, 56
Egypt, 10, 38, 54, 56, 57, 61
empire, 12–13, 34, 54–7
entertainment, 34–7, 39–42, 54
Epidaurus, 39–42
Erechtheum, 48–9
Eros, 7, 58
Euphorbus, 20
Euripides, 39, 62
Eurystheus, 20
festivals, 36–7, 39
fish and fishing, 30, 34, 35
food, 12, 22, 30, 32, 33, 34–5
footwear, 28, 32, 46
frescoes, 9, 11, 62
friezes, 48, 51, 62
funerals, 22
Furies, 20

G

Geometric period, 7, 46, 60
girls, 24, 25, 26, 29
gods, 9, 10, 13, 14, 18–19, 26, 36, 39, 44, 46, 56, 60, 61
gold, 10, 12, 29, 46, 48

government and law, 16–17, 38, 54
grapes, 30–1, 34
Greek orders, 49

H

Hades, 22, 23
health, 44–5
Hector, 20
Helen of Troy, 10
Hellenistic Age, 6, 7, 54–5, 61
Hephaestus, 19, 46, 56
Hera, 19
Heracles, 20, 22, 42, 52, 61
herbs, 34, 44
Hermes, 18, 20
Herodotus, 51, 62
Hesiod, 28, 62
Hesperides, 20–1
Hestia, 18
hetairai, 34–5
Hippocrates, 44, 45, 63
Homer, 11, 63
homes, 24–5, 60
hoplites, 50, 53
hunting, 52, 61

I–L

Ionic order, 49, 63
iron, 30, 46
Isthmian Games, 36, 37
Italy, 10, 12, 54, 56–7
ivory, 10, 48
javelin throwing, 37
jewellery, 11, 28, 29, 46, 60
juries, 16
Kimon, 17
Knossos, 9
legends see myths and legends
Linear A, 8, 63
Linear B, 27, 63
looms, 24, 63
Lydia, 33, 63

M

Macedonia, 52–3, 54, 56
marble, 8, 19, 46, 48, 51, 60
marriage, 24
masks (drama), 39–40
medicine, 44–5
Medusa, 20, 55
meeting places, 12, 32–3
men, 24, 28, 29, 32, 35, 44, 50
Menelaus, 10, 20
merchants, 30, 32
migration, 12–13

Minoan civilisation, 7, 8–9, 60
Minotaur, 9
Mount Olympus, 18–19
Mount Parnassus, 13
Muses, 26, 27
music, 26, 27, 30, 34, 36, 53
Mycenae, 6, 7, 8, 9, 10–11, 23, 27, 60
myths and legends, 6, 9, 10, 11, 18–23, 51

N–O

navy, 50–1
Nemean Games, 36, 37
nymphs, 20, 63
Odysseus, 7, 21, 22
olives, 31, 34
Olympic Games, 36–7
oracles, 13, 63
oratory, 16–17
ostracism, 17

P

Pan, 19
Paris, 10
Parthenon, 48, 58, 61
Pegasus, 20
Peloponnesian War, 50, 51
Pericles, 14, 45, 58, 63
Persephone, 23
Perseus, 20
Persia, 14, 52, 54
Persian Wars, 50–1
phalanx, 53
Pheidias, 48, 61, 63
Philip II of Macedon, 14, 52, 53
philosophy, 38, 43, 44, 63
Phoenicians, 27
Piraeus, 14–15
Plato, 38, 63
play, 24, 25
poetry, 11, 20, 27, 36
Poseidon, 18
pottery, 8, 10, 11, 46–7, 59, 60
priests/priestesses, 30, 44, 48
Ptolemy dynasty, 54
Pythagoras, 38, 43, 63
Pythian Games, 36, 37

R–S

red-figure ware, 47, 63
religion, 13, 24, 33, 57
see also gods
Renaissance, 59
River Styx, 22–3
Roman orders, 49

Rome, 54, 56–7
sacrifices, 18, 33, 36, 44
satyrs, 19, 63
Schliemann, Heinrich, 10, 11, 63
science, 38, 43–5
sculpture, 8, 12, 13, 20, 54, 60–1
seafaring, 6–7, 8–9, 14–15
Seleucus, 54
shipwrecks, 58–9, 60
sirens, 21
slaves, 16, 24, 25, 28, 30, 31, 32, 33, 35, 36, 46
Socrates, 38, 43, 63
Sophocles, 39, 42, 63
Sparta, 14, 15, 26, 32, 50
sport, 36–7, 52
statues, 18, 28, 48–9, 54, 58, 60–1
symposiums, 34, 35

T

Tartarus, 22
temples, 12, 13, 14, 15, 18, 44, 46, 48–9, 57, 58, 60
theatres, 39–42, 54
Thebes, 14
Thucydides, 51, 63
tombs, 22, 23, 60
trade, 6, 8, 10, 12, 14–15, 34
triremes, 50, 58, 63
Trojan horse, 10–11
Trojan War, 10, 11, 20, 51
Troy, 10–11, 21
Tuscan order, 49
tyrants, 16

U–Z

Underworld, 21, 22–3
voting, 16, 17
walled cities, 10, 11, 14
warfare, 14, 20, 36, 50–1
warships, 50–1
water, 24, 32, 33
weapons, 9, 10, 46, 53
weaving and spinning, 24, 28, 29, 32
wheat, 30, 34
wine making, 30–1
women, 24, 28, 29, 30, 32, 33, 34–5, 36, 39, 44, 51
wool, 28, 29
work, 30–1, 46–7
writing, 8, 12, 26–7, 58
Zeus, 18, 20, 23, 36, 52, 54, 57

Picture Credits

(t=top, b=bottom, l=left, r=right, c=centre, F=front, C=cover, B=back, Bg=background)
AKG, London, 36bc (Akademie der Bildenden Kuenste, Vienna/E. Lessing), 17bl (American School of Classical Studies, Athens), 9c, 9tl, 34bcl, 63cr (Archaeological Museum, Herakleion/E. Lessing), 19tcl (Archaeological Museum, Nauplion), 20cl (Badisches Landesmuseum, Karlsruhe), 14bc (British Museum), 33br (British Museum/E. Lessing), 48bc (J. Hios), 54bl (Israel Museum, Jerusalem/E. Lessing), 32cl (Kunsthistorisches Museum, Vienna/E. Lessing), 9tr, 20bl, 24bl, 24c, 34bl, 35bc, 38bcl, 38bl, 45tc, 62cl (The Louvre/E. Lessing), 51tl (Musee Vivenel, Compiegne), 19tc, 38c (Museo Nazionale Romano delle Terme, Rome/E. Lessing), 10bl (National Archaeological Museum, Athens), 21bl, 52tl (National Museum of Archaeology, Naples/E. Lessing), 59tr (Palazzo Salviati, Florence/E. Lessing), 54c (Pergamon Museum, Berlin), 23bc (Staatliche Antikensammlungen und Glyptothek, Munich/E. Lessing), 44tl. Ancient Art & Architecture Collection, 16br, 52tc (R. Sheridan), 15bl, 32tr, 39bc, 45cr. Austral International, 34tc (M. Friedel). Australian Picture Library, 11br, 40tl, 48tl (D. Ball), 9cl,

55cr (ET Archive), 57cr (ET Archive/Antalya Museum), 13cr, 39tr, 46tl (ET Archive/Archaeological Museum, Ferrara), 52b (ET Archive/Archaeological Museum, Istanbul), 39cl, 56bl, 57tr, 58bc (ET Archive/British Museum), 43br (ET Archive/Capitoline Museum, Rome), 14bl (ET Archive/Staatliche Glyptothek, Munich), 58tr (D. & J. Heaton). The Bridgeman Art Library, 20tr, 29cr, 31br, 33tc, 47br, 48bl, 50tr, 57bc, 61bl, 61cl (British Museum), 15bc (City of Bristol Museum & Art Gallery), 7bcr (Fitzwilliam Museum, University of Cambridge), 1, 7br, 19tl, 46cl, 62bl (Freud Museum, London), 27tl, 52cl, 54cl (Giraudon/The Louvre), 61tr (Lauros-Giraudon/The Louvre), 7cr, 23bl, 36tc (The Louvre), 10tl, 11cr, 23br, 61tl, 62cl (National Archaeological Museum, Athens), 47bc (Vatican Museums & Galleries). British Museum, 8tl, 12bc, 12tl, 12tr, 13tc, 22bl, 22cl, 24br, 24tc, 27bl, 28bl, 28c, 29tr, 30bl, 30cl, 30tl, 36bl, 44cl, 46bl, 60bl, 61br. C. M. Dixon, 51tc (Argos Museum, Greece), 39c, 42tr (British Museum), 46tr. The Granger Collection, 7tcr, 7tr, 8c, 11bcr, 11tc, 16tc, 20tl, 27tr, 36cl, 42tc, 58bl. The Image Bank, 58tl (S. Dee), 57bl (J. Zalon). National Archaeological Museum, Athens, 36tl, 37br, 60cr, 60tr. Scala, 8/9b, 60br, 60cl (National Museum, Athens), 39bl, 42tl. Werner Forman Archive, 28tl, 33tl (Acropolis Museum, Athens), 58cl (Bardo Museum, Tunisia), 18tr, 25bl, 34tl, 51cl (British Museum), 18cl.

Illustration Credits

Paul Bachem, 22/23t, 36/37c, 63bcr. Kenn Backhaus, 6/7c, 12cl, 20/21c. Chris Forsey, 3, 10/11c, 24/25c, 32/33c, 32bl. Adam Hook/Bernard Thornton Artists, UK, 14/15t, 39–42c, 39/40b, 50/51c, 51tr, 62tcr. Christa Hook/Bernard Thornton Artists, UK, 2, 4bl, 4br, 26/27c, 26/27t, 34/35c. Janet Jones, 5bc, 5cr, 16/17c, 16tl, 16bl, 38/43c, 38cl, 43tr, 46/47c, 62bcl, 62tl, 63br. Avril Makula, 43cr. Iain McKellar, 12/13c, 48/49c, 49tr, 49br, 56/57c, 58/59c. Steve Noon/Garden Studio, 30/31c, 31bc. Matthew Ottley, 52/53c, 53tr. Sharif Tarabay/Garden Studio, 5tl, 28/29c, 29br, 44/45c, 44b. Steve Trevaskis, 4cl, 18/19c, 19cr. Rod Westblade, endpapers, icons. Ann Winterbotham, 54/55c, 55tr.

Cover Credits

AKG, London, Bg (Pergamon Museum, Berlin). Austral International, BCbr (M. Friedel). The Bridgeman Art Library, FCtl (The Louvre). British Museum, FCtr. Chris Forsey, FCc. Adam Hook/Bernard Thornton Artists, UK, BCtl.